CASCADE EXPERIMENT: *Selected Poems*

Poetry

Dance Script With Electric Ballerina
Palladium
Powers Of Congress
Sensual Math
Felt

Essays

Feeling as a Foreign Language:
  The Good Strangeness of Poetry

CASCADE EXPERIMENT

Selected Poems

ALICE FULTON

W. W. NORTON & COMPANY

NEW YORK | LONDON

Manufacturing by Courier Westford
Book design by JAM Design
Production manager: Anna Oler

Library of Congress Cataloging-in-Publication Data

Fulton, Alice, date.
Cascade experiment : selected poems / Alice Fulton.— 1st ed.
p. cm.
ISBN 0-393-05928-6 (hardcover)
I. Title.
PS3556.U515A6 2004
811'.54—dc22

2003028124

ISBN 0-393-32762-0 (pbk)

W. W. Norton & Company, Inc., 500 Fifth Avenue, New York, N.Y. 10110
www.wwnorton.com

W. W. Norton & Company Ltd., Castle House, 75/76 Wells Street, London W1T 3QT

1 2 3 4 5 6 7 8 9 0

for Hank

Contents

ACKNOWLEDGMENTS

Dance Script With Electric Ballerina was first published by the University of Pennsylvania Press, Philadelphia, in 1983 as the winner of the Associated Writing Programs Award in Poetry. It was reprinted by the University of Illinois Press, Urbana and Chicago, in 1996. Selections from that edition are reprinted here by permission of the University of Illinois Press.

Palladium was published by the University of Illinois Press, Urbana and Chicago, in 1986 as the winner of the National Poetry Series Competition. Selections from *Palladium* are reprinted by permission of the University of Illinois Press.

Powers Of Congress, first published by David R. Godine, Boston, in 1990, was reprinted by Sarabande Books, Louisville, in 2001. Selections from that edition are reprinted here by permission of Sarabande Books.

from

DANCE SCRIPT
WITH ELECTRIC
BALLERINA

1978 - 1981

What I Like

Friend—the face I wallow toward
through a scrimmage of shut faces.
Arms like towropes to haul me home, aide-
memoire, my lost childhood docks, a bottled ark
in harbor. *Friend*—I can't forget
how even the word contains an *end*.
We circle each other in a scared bolero,
imagining stratagems: postures and imposters.
Cold convictions keep us solo. I ahem
and hedge my affections. Who'll blow the first kiss,
land it like the lifeforces we feel
tickling at each wrist? It should be easy
easy to take your hand, whisper down this distance
labeled hers or his: what I like about you is

Two Cries & A Clutch

This boy liked me once:
two cries & a clutch.
Young blood, thin as a pick
he broke my lips & woke my tongue.
His contrary motions roughed
the nubs of my spine. I sharpened
my heart on his.

Now he keeps another nymph
in his guitar case: venus
plucked & scrubbed. He needs it
very clean. I need something more
than twenty toes twisting
beneath a sheet.

His shaggy hair's gone
lean. Mine's gray
as filaments: I own
this forty-watt glow, this season—
my flesh melts down, I stick
to chairs & churn
the words. His music
goes & comes. Where is the knowing
we sewed up years ago?

When we rubbed in the wet
storeways of Graytown, U.S.A.
police cars smoothed by
in the groundsteam, rain
made a heart murmur: *mine*
one of us said to one of us.
We didn't speak to strangers then.

Yours & Mine

Through your lens the sequoia swallowed me
like a dryad. The camera flashed & forgot.
I, on the other hand, must practice my absent-
mindedness, memory being awkward as a touch
that goes unloved. Lately your eyes have shut
down to a shade more durable than skin's. I know you
love distance, how it smooths. You choose an aerial view,
the city angled to abstraction, while I go for the close
exposures: poorly-mounted countenances along Broadway,
the pigweed cracking each hardscrabble backlot.
It's a matter of perspective: yours is to love me
from a block away & mine is to praise the grain-
iness that weaves expressively: your face.

My Diamond Stud

He'll be a former cat burglar
because I have baubles
to lose. I'll know him
by the black
carnation he's tossing:
heads, he takes me,
stems, the same. Yes,
he'll be a hitchhiker at this
roller-rink I frequent, my diamond
stud who'll wheel up shedding
sparks & say "*Ecoutez
bé-bé.* I'm a member
of a famous folded trapeze
act. My agility is legend, etc."
keeping his jeweler's eye on
my gold fillings. He'll know
what I really want: whipping
me with flowers, his fingers' grosgrain
sanded smooth, raw
to my every move. For our tryst
we'll go to travel-folder heaven
& buff-puff each other's
calluses in valentine tubs.
He'll swindle the black heart
between my thighs
dress me up in ultra-
suede sheaths, himself
in naugahyde. No,
leather. He'd never
let anything touch him
that wasn't once alive.

Second Sight

If I could fire a song so strong men cut themselves,
I won't say only when shaving, would you
be moved? Or say I dyed
my hair an alibi of sweet and twenty
would the odds improve? After we kissed
I wore my mouth like a neon bowtie for days, even
pleased with Times Square's holiday displays:
those electric devils pimping their winks.
Your voice sparks in me yet: a red signal leaping
up a radio tower, the stars chattering in light
years. One kiss, the kind that commonly dazzles
a jukebox to croon, but with me still in continuum,
its second-sight like a candle's: clairvoyant
tongue quickening the night.

Life Above The Permafrost

All winter the trees tossed in their coma.
Beneath them fields unrolled
like a pallet. Snow came,
the universal donor, the connective
in all the ready metaphors:
sky coarse as hotel linen,
bedsheets the half-white of rice
paper. That kinship.

Prone as the land,
I wanted each day to start
the way the body starts in sleep: a reflex
of sun, mimosa explosions. Not
the window's slow tap of the sky,
light rising like sap
in maples, and even the maples
warted with sparrows
too frigid to fly South.
Those trees needed wild flamingos, at least,
to break their drowse.

In bed, my nails raked
the chenille spread, its whitework
like a mulch of snow. Snug as a corm
in its coldframe, the heart
shied from my five-fingered tongs.

Now there are parasol garnishes
on the rum drinks of summer, Adirondack
chairs with wind in the slats. Your arms band
me like a migratory bird. I think,
this must be life
above the permafrost. The raised candle-

wicking of the quilt
cornrows our skin. Our fingers braid
like aerial roots.

You make me want
to stop tending relics in my head,
that well-stocked potter's field:
just listen to the insects'
adenoidal plainsong all day long,
enamored of the keynote, the tonic.

The Great Aunts Of My Childhood

Buns harden like pomanders
at their napes, their famous good
skin is smocked like cloth.
Stained glass wrings out the light
and the old tub claws the oilcloth.
Kit makes cups of bitter cocoa
or apricot juice that furs my throat.
Mame dies quietly in the bedroom.

She pressed the gold watch
into my hands, wanted me to take
her middle name at confirmation:
Zita, Saint of Pots and Pans;
but I chose Theresa, the Little Flower,
a face in the saint's book
like a nosegay. I chose this

blonde room sprouting jade
plants, electric necessities
and nights that turn
my nipples to cloves
till dawn pours in like washwater
to scrub the floors
with harsh yellow soap.

The Gone Years

Night pockets the house
in a blue
muffle the color
of my father's Great Depression.
I see him move
over the snow, leaving
the snow unmoved.
The snow has no imagination.

My mother and I shuffle by
each other as if we were
the dead, speechless
breathers at windows done in black
oilcloth tacked down by stars.

"It's fair that his clothes be worn
out as he was." She irons them
for distant cousins, the tattersalls
sending up a hush
beneath her hands.

Through January's flannel
nights she turns old
stories over and over,
letting the gone
years hug her
with his long wool arms.

Toward Clairvoyance

Dust is the only secret—
                    —EMILY DICKINSON, POEM 166

You hold all our home truths, nil-colored one.
Silk lingerie and high-rag notebooks are pilfered
sooner or later to your dumb dimension.
My mother railed against you daily
with my dead father's undershirts
in hand. But nothing flusters your calm
quantum for long. You'll allow
the piano its shine and move to stifle
a brass candlestick. Still

I like to think there's a speck
in me that couldn't be conscripted
just as a wind or river holds
your residue yet is always
breath or wetness. Lackluster stuff,
our throats close in your midst—we go wheezing
toward clairvoyance. Other presences
reveal their reasons clearly
to the senses. But you are most discreet and least
exotic, slipping your scant
cataracts beneath our lids each night. I hear

a voice in you like voices hidden
under hands, low conversations seeping
through the door's warped jamb. And the dust
a hundred miles away is your verbatim. Dullard!
who never spawns or swats
a single life, whose only racket

is our comeuppance, you lie
in ambush like a future
fact: a flat world
waiting to be
round.

Between The Apple And The Stars

Newton did not shew the cause of the apple falling, but he shewed a similitude between the apple and the stars.
—SIR D'ARCY WENTWORTH THOMPSON

By now we know
the portents: an apple falls
in a plague year,
a star rises
in the East.
A premature birth,

Christmas 1642.
"Small enough
to fit in a quart mug,"
his mother said. So feeble
he needed a brace
to raise his head.

Once after studying the sun
it took three days
of darkness to revive
his eyes. Then for months
when he thought *sun*
its ghost rose
on his retina.

But more than laws,
he sought the divine.
One Stone
to undo the skimpy differences
in matter: bread to flesh,
wine to blood, percolating wild

elixirs; even at the end
longing for "another shake
at the moon, another touch
at metals." Now gravity

lies passive as quicksand
under the jet.
But what of the Stone
with its "beravishing
smells, apparitions
of angels?" The scientist passes
a hand like a wand over
the wondrous button. The Stone

one day will render
all vibrancies
singular
as light. So apples
float from trees
and stars ripen
and die at ground
speed.

Dance Script With Electric Ballerina

Here I am on this ledge again,
my body's five rays singing,
limbering up for another fling
with gravity. It's true,
I've dispensed with some conventions.
If you expected sleeping
beauty sprouting from a rococo
doughnut of tulle, a figurine
fit to top a music box, you might want
your money back. I'll take a getup
functional as light:
feet bright and precise as eggbeaters,
fingers quick as switch-
blades and a miner's lamp for my tiara.
You've seen kids on Independence Day, waving
sparklers to sketch their initials on the night?
Just so, I'd like to leave a residue
of slash and glide, a trace-
form on the riled air.
Like an action painter, tossing form on space
instead of oil on cloth,
I'm out to disprove the limited
orbit of fingers, swing some double-jointed
miracles, train myself to hover above ground
longer than the pinch of time allowed.

This stingy escarpment leaves so little
room to move!
But perhaps that's for the best. Despite brave talk
of brio and ballon, spectators prefer
gestures that don't endanger
body and soul. Equilibrium
is so soothing—while any strain is a reminder

of the pain that leads to grace:
muscles clenched like teeth to the shin, swollen
hubs of shoulder, ankle, wrist, and knee,
toes brown as figs from the clobbering
of poundage. In this game, lightness is all.
Here's another trick. When passing the critics
turn sideways to expose less
surface. Think like a knife
against the whetstone sneers: *unsympathetic*
in several minds   flat and hollow
at the core   shabby   too
flaccid   polishes off her pirouettes with
too assertive
a flick   ragged barbaric hysterical
needs to improve
her landings   technique   bullies
the audience into paying
attention   in short
does not really get around   lacking
assurance authority fluency restraint roundness
of gesture   something
of the air and manner of those who are ballerinas
by right rather than
assumption: one will say
I'm mildly impressed
by her good line and high extensions.

I can sense the movement
notators' strobe vision
picking the bones of flux into
positions. Can't they see the gulf
between gestures as a chance
to find clairvoyance—
a gift that thrives on fissures
between then and now and when?
If a complex network, a city, say

could be filmed for a millennium
and the footage shown
so in three hours it woke
from huts to wired shining,
its compressed assembling would be like this
dance: these air patterns
where I distill the scribbling moves
that start at birth
and dissolve in death.

Till then I'm signing space
in leaps angular and brief
as an electrocardiograph's beat.
Now as I settle on an ending
posture: my chest heaves,
joints shift, eyes dart—
and even at a stand-
still, I'm dancing.

Diminuendo

There is another sky
and then another, in smooth
segue. The windows are flush
with its thick fortissimo
or spacious blue,
with its one sun,
open as a whole note.

And all its moods just
suit me: the self-effacing
fall sky, gray and receptive
as tape to my voice, or luminous
in spring, with that glow
all gems borrow strictly from it.

Last night I heard a woman ask
a chance acquaintance, "Would you
hold me?" and thought
That's a question I'd trust
only to a lover
like the sky: too composed
for a quick or sour
motion. Its steady

glissando of light
never leaves anyone for long.
Maybe that's why
I like to lie under summer's
wide sun and I like this waiting

for another sky:
a white sky that tints the world
its shade through snow's dim-

inuendo. A sky
that falls, touching me, at last
as if it too were being
diminished, when the blank below
matches the blank above
and the whole horizon goes.

from

PALLADIUM

1982 - 1985

Babies

born gorgeous with nerves, with brains
the pink of silver polish or
jellyfish wafting ornately
through the body below.
An invertebrate cooing
on the mother
tongue shushes and lulls them into thinking
all is well. As they grow they learn

salvage: tear-out
guides to happiness say apologies can outshine
lies, guilt be lickspittled from their lives, bad
glycerined to good. Like a child's first school pencils
in their formal brilliance
and sharp new smells, they grow and lie

as lovers. Maybe one cries
the wrong name and the night skinning
them pleasantly alive
leaps away in shards.
Then it's time for restitution:
a tin of homebaked,
holding gingham safety, fetal
as the light through mason jars of beets and brine,
or jewelry, clasping and unclasping
aisles of fluorescence from great department stores,
a distracting plenitude, and tempting.

Still, the beloved may stay bitter as an ear
the tongue pressed
into, unwanted.
And the word *end:* spiney, finally-formed,

indents them and is
understood. They learn

the hard way as hurts
accrue, and the brain is cratered as a rock
by rain that fell ages past
on unprotected mud. An insult keeps
despite apologies. When it vaporizes at last,
its space fills with grains that harden
to a fossil shaped exactly
like the insult.
They grow up when they know that

sometimes
only a gesture responsive as a heart-
shaped parachute above a jump
a life depends on
to be perfect
the first time will ever do.

Nugget And Dust

My father clipped coupons at the kitchen table,
his numismatic faith burnished like currency
in the safe. He was able
to give himself in visible ways: my birth-
day present, the Buick
Skylark, the silk
he wrapped us in against neuralgia, loyalties
moral as 11th-hour tales
in *True*, the only magazine he took.
Meanwhile, I was full of prim
insurrections, a maximalist
on a shoestring. How could I

admit I withdrew from him
as from a too-gentle thing I wanted to live
forever? I couldn't stand the forthcoming
sadness. Love, if true, is tacit.
It accumulates, nugget and dust, arcade of sweet
exchange. I argued the self-
evidence of all enhancements.
Yet we were camouflaged. I told lies
in order to tell the truth,
something I still do. It was hard

to imagine a world in tune
without his attention
to its bewildering filters, emergency
brakes, without his measured tread. Diligent world,
silly world! where keys turn and idiot lights
signal numinous privations.

The Body Opulent

Mr. Silver owned a steel plant
and manipulated auras on the outskirts
of Detroit: a faith healer.
Perhaps he could heal
mine. Through subdivisions trim and brown
as bouillon cubes, defoliated zones,
where heavy machinery depreciated, I took my heart.

The waiting room contained a cloudy sky
made finite in linoleum, a kind of American marble.
Whatever lured me here?
A month ago I'd plunged into a double-dark nothing
like sleep since sleep gives dividends
of dream, free wake-ups.
Doctors pursued the elusive
verdict, their spooky machines
awhirr with purpose. Their glowing dyes
showed fiery tributaries ribboning
my heart: arabesques of argon violet
crosshatched in patterns so complex
they seemed quite random. It would take some faith
to unravel all that
bafflement! Was it heretical
to expect things from this
world? To want to live
forever in the cells' jewel glut, the body opulent,
a squirming heaven in each fist.

Mr. Silver spoke first of psychics with the power
to bend metal, supernormally
light lamps two miles away,
draw like famous artists, and speed

the growth of seeds. Though he could do none of these,
I sensed a Yankee optimism
when he mentioned his ability to diagnose and treat
disease. "Never mind preachers
finding devils under everybody's skin.
Some things are beyond our knowing.
It's important to believe." When I agreed
he seemed relieved. "All right, sports fans,
let's see if these success stories go beyond
conjecture," he said. I was to close my eyes
and meditate on something pleasant
while he mediated over me.

Though I tried to snag my mind on sweetness,
I kept thinking
this is America. And I hadn't told anyone
where I was going.
He put his hands around my neck and squeezed.
Each cell got busy, singing
the dawnsong of its name;
my body suddenly felt worth its weight
in light, as if I held the sky
above an earthquake—the magenta glow
made by electric fields and shifting
plates—inside each artery and vein.
After thirty minutes he backed off
to give the news. "It's true, you have a cardiac
screw loose. But I'll tell you what
to do. *Smile.* Meditate
like you did tonight. Remember
you don't have to kiss anybody's fanny.
You're going to be all right."
By way of farewell, blessing, or epiphany,
he feelingly recited Kipling's "If."
Then his flashlight led me through a maze
of cold rolled metal, polychromed partitions.

Outside, the night was laced with bright fillips
of pidgin English: Glassbenders,
in bins among transformers, standing
burners, the din and smell of lightning,
formed these Lifesavers and double helices of neon,
an old-fashioned, hard to stack, quickly cracking
stuff. They vacuumed each tube of impurities, primed
the inside with hot-colored phosphor, painted
the spaces between letters black. They burned
themselves welding adrenaline messages
into night: "La Chambre: Exotic
Dancers," "Warsaw Foot-Long." "Elijah's

Hellenic Den" looked the most respectable.
When I opened the door, a waiter raised a platter
of flames. "Opa!" the patrons roared
as if their lungs were made of silk
wrapped round a shout.
Still hoping for signs and wonders,
I thought it might mean Health or Life, an omen
of survival. "It's just something we say.
It means like olé. It don't mean
nothing," the waiter told me.
The appetizers were dark and shiny; the wine local,
from grapes grown in the Motor
City, going by its nose of Pennzoil and Prestone.
A dubious sustenance. Yet I swallowed it
like gospel that somehow did me good.
I was lucky, then,

under the enormous torque
of midwest sky, to find my Nova
in the lot, to drive past emblems
galvanizing night: the golden arches,
spirals, labyrinths, and flags; the logos

placed like halos
above service stations—Mobil,
Gulf, and Shell; the freeway's glowing
dot and dash, a path
of crumbs to follow home.

603 West Liberty St.

Captivity is Consciousness—
So's Liberty—
    —EMILY DICKINSON, POEM 649

They said here, take this,
and I was handed Faith like shelter, food, matter-

of-factly. I learned
about Sin: a tarry fetish, a binge, the devil's stretch

limo, turbine
of desire; and Penance: the bargain

struck, the scrub of absolution through murmurous
screens; indulgence and the State of Grace

entered then: its starry promise, divine
parole select as sterling. Frisked

of aberrations I felt insipid—
a dimestore creche. Evidently the soul

flickered like a flimsy version of the body:
born whole, then fractured

by venial, mortal flaws. I wondered why I lived
in warmth and weight

unlike the air. I touched
myself, tentative, and questioned

futures inlaid with *forever*. At best I could believe
in the quantum world's array of random

without chaos, its multiplicity—a crown
of right responses!—alone seemed moral.

It was faith
like a gate: earthbound, yet

permeable. I could go through.
It was faith, if not exactly

mountain-moving. Not the kind that moves pilgrims
through austere ranges: rumpled

hills in Nepal, the airy gray
of pumice, as if the whole land-

scape levitated. Those pilgrims walk
because they know

the Crystal Mountain is a tent-
pole holding up the heavens. They believe this

because they believe that
100 years ago a white conch shell

fell and a yogi flew on his snow
lion to pierce the capstone, slinging rain-

bows round the clouds. An event
unseen, but taken on

Faith, which is itself in-
visible. It grows in the open

stadiums under mercury
vapors lashed to derricks. It floats

a bristling star above the born-
again, the preacher with one hand raised

to shield or summon. It spins
each soul like a gyroscope and where

it points, we go.

Everyone Knows The World Is Ending

Everyone knows the world is ending.
Everyone always thought so, yet
here's the world. Where fundamentalists flick slideshows
in darkened gyms, flash endtime mess-
ages of bliss, tribulation
through the trembling bleachers: Christ will come
by satellite TV, bearing millennial weather
before plagues of false prophets and real locusts
botch the cosmic climate—which ecologists predict
is already withering from the green-
house effect as fossil fuels seal in
the sun's heat and acid rains
give lakes the cyanotic blues.

When talk turns this way, my mother speaks in memories,
each thought a focused mote in the apocalypse's
iridescent fizz. She is trying to restore a world
to glory, but the facts shift with each telling
of her probable gospel. Some stories have been
trinkets in my mind since childhood, yet what clings is not
how she couldn't go near the sink
for months without tears when her mother died,
or how she feared she wouldn't get her own
beribboned kindergarten chair, but the grief
in the skull like radium
in lead, and the visible dumb love like water
in crystal, at one with what holds it. The triumph

of worlds beyond words. Memory entices because ending is
its antonym. We're here to learn
the earth by heart and everything is crying
mind me, mind me! Yet the brain selects and shimmers
to a hand on skin while numbing the constant

stroke of clothes. Thoughts frame and flash
before the dark snaps back: the dress with lace tiers
she adored and the girl with one just like it,
the night she woke to see my father
walk down the drive and the second she remembered
he had died. So long as we keep chanting the words
those worlds will live, but just
so long, so long, so long. Each instant waves
through our nature and is nothing.
But in the love, the grief, under and above
the mother tongue, a permanence
hums: the steady mysterious
the coherent starlight.

The New Affluence

Let me say "we" for I am not alone in this
desire to live
where the land is neither dramatically flat
nor high, where it snows enough
to keep the world
the bitter white of aspirin.

People with such needs grew up
snow-belted, rust-belted,
in towns like mine where muscle
cars dragged down Main Streets
and the fountain's aigrettes outside
the Miss Troy Diner offered welcome
hits of pink and blue in a landscape
largely the noncolor of lard.

Our choice: to love or hate
the slight reprieves from plainness: the fractious birds,
the scrappy trees, and most of all
the things that didn't live or breathe—
factories tearing up the sky with smoke,
tugboats sweet as toys
along the poisoned river.
A budget, if not famine, our lives.
Perhaps a sweepstakes, with prizes so slight
no one cared to enter. We wouldn't have become
susceptible to the tag ends, seconds,
as-is of experience, given better
scenery. We wouldn't have gotten this idea
that happiness is mined like ore from rock,
through efforts of imagination. We, the poor,
but not in spirit, we
the not especially blessed,

who, working cold hours at dull jobs,
drank, gambled, went mad, or grew
anomalous as water—
a compound that expands while freezing.

Disciples of steam and dust,
we take pleasure in considering
the glaciers beginning
in the clouds, the picnic springing up
around the subatomic
particles others call the vacuum.
Our sensory thresholds—the nerve centers
that decide what to let us know—let us know
too much, which makes us terrible
at parties: we seize upon the slight
conflicting tics in idle chitchat,
the wayward rift behind a smile.
It's exhausting, and a social hindrance.
Twitchers, fainters, cringelings,

I'm here to say you'd like it
where I live. In this converted bakery
everything's left to the imagination:
the golden smell of molten sugar, the customers
gazing at pastries baked from scratch
into planes and turrets
fanciful as women's hats.
A tub of lard, sealed and dated 1900,
was the one remaining trace
of baking and we left it
sealed, imagining a cache
of rancid snow within.
The local paper gives advice to liven up our days:
"Colored towels add eye-spice. Look for cotton
run-on sales. A blub-blub of vinegar
adds zip to many dishes. Try it, it's terrif."

It was the absence of spectacular views that made us
see the sparrow hopping warily,
as if the ground were strewn with acid.
(Medieval legend says it hissed
"He lives," to Roman soldiers at Calvary,
for which God bound its feet forever
with supernatural string.)
Lacking diversions, we've turned furtive
in order to observe it. We toss crumbs
while light pours crisp as seltzer, as peppermint
oil through air.

The hyacinths need these cold weeks
to grow into fragrant vases
full only of themselves, their particular
being, like everything else.
So summer comes
to meet us. Soon children
will sell chances on rocks and leaves
from sidewalk stands.
Children! They think these things
are valuable. And we always buy.

Fugitive

Stars, though famous
by definition, are anonymous
in spirit. Unlike boys,
the star did not demand
a certain level of response.
She could flip
through rows of him without feeling
blunt. She imagined that he imagined her
and that was how she could exist.
Like a captive crisscrossed
from room to room across a nation,
she had trouble telling
one place from another.
For instance, she believed the same class
had been going on for years
throughout her school.
Priests were mixed messages; their words
formed a gray frost
on her face like breath on a wind-
shield. In class, she wished up gardens
off the straight and narrow
toward water events, stone holes
spouting, cherry trees
that drew things
to them and disposed of them.
A mildly active perfection: hundreds of goldfish
flitting like polished nails
in ponds. Or a mossy house
with walls of water—so risky
no one would stay for long.
The days were held
breaths let out
with irritation when she got home,

as if someone there had clamped
a hand over her mouth.
At night she clipped
articles about the star
and read. Books understood her. She read
how you could lose
a limb and still feel it
reaching. But her experience was, as ever,
opposite: you could keep a body and feel
you'd lost it. She had
long nails and always did
everything with them.
But to play the star's
songs on guitar she had to
clip the white tips.
The strings left pink
incisions backed by fugitive
stings, surprising
after years of not touching. She began to dream
the auditory dreams
of the blind, to read in the dark
and with her hands, like them.

Scumbling

Absolved, face to the wall, alive only
in fact. It was always evening
in my head, an evening of thoughts
cool as sheets. His skin
made its silk sound, no
two glissandos alike. A fine fear
streaked through. Let somebody else
sponge up those tremors.
My reserve circled, imperial
as the inside of a pearl. All night
I pretended night was an unruly
day. I pretended
my voice. I pretended my hair. I pretended
my friend. But there it was—"I"—
I couldn't get rid of that.
What could I do but let it learn
to tremble? So I watched feelings hover
over like the undersides
of waterlilies: long serpentines
topped by nervous almost-
sunny undulations. I had to learn
largo. I had to trust
that two bodies scumbling
could soften
one another. I had to
let myself be gone
through, do it in the arbitrary light
tipping and flirting
with seldom-seen surfaces.

Works On Paper

A thrilling wilderness of bio-
morphic script, you said
my letters scared you. And it's even worse
in person: pink oil of lipprints, unnervingly organic
Hi's, those kisses like collusions. For a moment
we vibrate like underwater stones.
What is this
windfall? We are not easily becalmed.
How you pull back
as if to deflect affection.
How I pull back, swear
to clothe myself
in jokes. Graft the properties of blandness

to the social handshake
and we'll have it: how to get through
this world intact. Placebos do
nicely—expressions never point
blank but fixed
like bets between grin and grimace.
What I work to know is whether passion,
roaring, snapping
its head, can be prelude
to entertainment, harmless as MGM's
old lion. And is seduction a science
or a pattern of cheap frills; can you make it
from a kit? What suave

impoverishments we chose.
And I can do it: fake
formality, dissemble
with the best, lady it
over lessers: Pick me!

Pick me! Of course not
to care, to keep
the heart complacent as a dumpling,
that's hard. What of emotions
that grow so steep they can't hold
shape and the pinnacle
leaps forward, breaking as it does
in waves? I'm afraid

those emotions keep us lonely.
I'm afraid there are no bribes
equal to the body-
guards. We love surface
articulation. And when we say
Abandon abandon we mean it
as a command. Here's an illustrative touch:

Delacroix, old realist, got so excited
entering a harem's room
he had to be calmed
down with sherbets. Passion! Maybe
it only works on paper. But once
in a well-lit room
I buried my face in the material,
shirting, that opened to darker emulsions, rich
scents unlike others as burnt umber's
unlike other colors. It was about expansion.
There were brief constellations
down the willing nerves,
an effulgence: worth it, worth it.

Palladium Process

I, a cloud
chamber. My face, a flag-
stone over feeling: if touched I knew
the indentation would fill slowly
as a hole in sand. I was islanded,
a nightingale that couldn't sing
while anybody watched, caged
in paper screens emitting a faint light,
the view through a glassine, scarcely
glanceable. Each day became a vacant lot
I trimmed with safety
scissors, blade by blade. Skirted, stalled,
in the realm between feeling and expression,
sensations fell to me as stones fall
down a well: the wait, the distant clink.
Joy, too, sank: sand in an hourglass,
gravity-tamped.
              Yet the mystery simmered:
Love and rage dried and piled up
like hay in stables that combusts
in tongues. It took angers, lovers,
to enfranchise me. There was this difficult rip-
cord! Then control scattered
as I edged toward expansion.
              When I came to life
as to a come-as-you-are
fiesta, wrongly dressed, my face
had the telltale patina of solitude,
the strangeness of statues
dragged from sunken holds.
And my happiness seemed silly
as a terrier's in a blizzard, chasing
every dizzy flake.

At last, the world surprised me:
I became a student
of surplus, moved by the ubiquitous, sometimes
broken roses, or the serious
hilarity of the stars. I started
at ordinary things
the way a 19th-century gentleman might
start at a glimpse of undraped
limb. Shivers. There were
dictionaries. There were tricks
of the light, dextrous
evanescent cathedrals, improvident
constructions, inventories
like the palladium inventories of
sun!

Peripheral Vision

for David Lehman

The window's a slow-moving liquid.
In it, the scientist sees another window
drifting, smaller,
larger, smaller. It is the opposite
structure rocking, or her own
structure or herself. Her colleagues watch

a film of their last field
trip. She's distracted
by their black and white extremities,
the ancillary hands and feet. What blooms
beneath their suits, snug
as guilt? Snug as God
in a hideaway heaven, chanting
standard tasks: observe, examine,
isolate.

The screen's a jungle.
On it, others study flirtatious affidavits:
the jeep's tracks mixed with the tiger's
four-toed flash.
They funnel white cloth
between trees, knowing a gauntlet
strongly felt but faintly

seen will spook the tiger
to the darts, the collar
with its battery-
driven signal. Once they have it
ticking, aerial tracking
charts its drift, antennas
on each wing

strut sounding loudest
when pointed toward kinetic
yellow. After canvasing negative space
for ages, the trackers should grow
eyes on stalks that fan the air and fasten
like stays to their domain. Seeing's

such a commemorative gesture. The scientist focuses
on the fiery valentine
that is the tiger's nose.
Is there a cover equal to the giveaway
signal? Does the thought admit regret,
resistance? The heart's a partisan,

but intellect, a stickler, wants to know
in what sense precisely
the tiger's burning bright.
The heart envisions God
in Greece, blasting gilt
from acroliths, exposing
wooden torsos belied by marble arms.
But the mind insists
the God of triangles would be
three-sided: we see what we want
to see. She knows that

glass is a skittery solid,
and film a chain of static frames,
that nature is unchanging,
though it does change. Driving
home, sun slices, horizontally, a line
of trees, or trees skate
past the rooted sun, or cars drift
by the steadfast sun and trees.
What will it be? When God is a round
centered everywhere,

a circumference found nowhere, expanding
the universe, building

new alloys from happenstance and junk.
So constancy won't hold
her. The pupil's noose fits
mornings shaped by matchstick
blinds, the dawn cracked into
even lines. But vision twists
galaxies through the window,

holistic. Her mind works
toward the marginal,
what's tentative but ready
to take on sound and color: the radio tower
underwired with subtle
stripes and flames, invisible leapaway
music bulleting to distant hit parades.

Fierce Girl Playing Hopscotch

You sway like a crane to the tunes of tossed stones.
I am what you made to live in
from what you had: hair matted as kelp, bad schools.

Oh, you will never know me. I wave and you go
on playing in the clouds
boys clap from erasers. I am the pebble
you tossed on the chalked space and war-
danced toward, one-leg two-leg, arms treading air.

In this, your future, waves rechristen the sea
after its tiny jeweled lives
that hiss "Us Us" to the shore all day.
Where's the kid called Kateydid? The moonfaced
Kewpiedoll? The excitable pouting
Zookie? The somber O-Be-Joyful?

Lost girl, playing hopscotch, I will do what you could.
Name of father, son, ghost. Cross my heart and hope.
While the sea's jewels build shells and shells
change to chalk and chalk to loam and gold
wheat grows where oceans teetered.

Obsessions

steady as the heat
bugs' drone, a rip of white
water too violent
to support much
life. *Only, only, only*
that's the song, self-
absorbed and hardly knowing

us. Meanwhile, our faces vibrate
with desires visible as the inner
workings of certain see-through fish.
How to be more
guarded? Our jaws move
precisely and silk issues
forth in double strands. We speak

in meshes accurate to a ruler's least
degree. Such eloquence, such craft!
Each facet of our fascination
expands. What's desired slips
from its true scale, becomes meta-
physical as a blown-up cell: an opalescence
of congealed light, a shimmering

edema. Blinding.
A close brush with attainment quite
undoes us. We feel
heavily unconscious, submerged in colors dense
as chloroform, distant
effervescent riffles, the roar of boulders in a whirlpool,
slight sandy agitations. If we get near

enough to touch
the desired feels unsettling,
on the fringe of foreign
elements: downy as an algal mat. Sometimes
wanting so unwisely is enough
to make us wish the sheeted surface would break
loose. We'd almost welcome ice

scours, a strict denuding, *only*:
under the numbness, lesser lives
still cling and fight—
one thousand to one
cubic inch. You'd think they counted
themselves dear. You'd think we encouraged
their drowsy, unseen births, breathed on them

said *treasure*.

Terrestrial Magnetism

Stars threatened you into feeling
negligible while susceptible
to connections, I saw many more
than two dippers riddling the sky.

Nights you'd leap down
from stellar atmospheres, wrap yourself
around me like a sari
as the lead guitar took his
solo. For the first time, I felt
singled out. I know you'd agree

that those letters written from faraway
gigs had the suspect sweetness of breath
mints, leaving me to guess what sour
moonlighting they covered,
and that losing you I lost

a language I couldn't stand
to have back, with words for need
obsessive as daylight,
a spectra glowing from all directions.

Together would we have fallen
into offices and sweated
under cubed light, would we
at day's end have gotten into better cars
than those we own and found without meaning
to we'd driven ourselves home?

I've spent years since
tracing the vapor formed between storm

and inner windows, sweeping the sky
for a star undigested by the dark, planet
perturbations, under the left breast, a heart.

Traveling Light

Every restaurant boarded up in softwood,
bars strung with tipsy blinkers, smudgefires
against the dusk-
like day: who could have imagined the light
toppling down, song you can see
over all? Or this salt breeze,
vital and teary as a drunken wake.
The kite store's ringed with stunted Christmas
trees like pathetic closed umbrellas.
This is the year we'll trim with shells.
The man who sells them tells us tales
of smuggling, of price wars over apple coral,
fluted clams. His hair branches and his skin
hardens as he speaks: part baobab, part pirate.
His shells—little bandana prints, green turbans—
are lovely, "droll" might be the word,
but tropical, not from Cape Cod.

It was ten years ago this season
my father died, leaving me odd
wisdoms concerning clip joints,
gypsies, toeroom, elocution,
and traveling light. I was twenty,
up to my elbows in developer,
acid, fixative: a microfilm
technician with few discernible skills.
What would he have made of this off-season
resort? Though he never lived to see it
I can hear him say "Don't worry,
Al, if the poetry don't go
I'll buy you your own beauty shop."
Yes, with sickly pink
smells, well-thumbed back issues

of *Hairdo* and a 3-D religious picture
that flickered between Mary and Jesus,
in tricky light revealing
the Blessed Mother with a beard.
He liked scenery, Kay Francis
movies and the fights. I guess,
like you, I never really knew him.

On the last visit I ambled to his room
with my dignified mini hiked up
in the back, flashing
unintentional ass to the joyous
orderlies. Befuddled by dripping
liquids, screens yielding twitchy lights
he said "What are we doing
in this carwash?" Then he thought he remembered
a long ago close call, when a canvas-topped jalopy
broke down in a Saratoga storm.
His hands froze first, then his flesh turned
dense as a snowman's. Only his brain kept
rolling. He knew he had no money.
The troopers took him to a sumptuous
hospital, and his eyes grew wondrous
as he raved and praised
the decor, the meals. "You can't imagine!
When I went to pay the nurses
said 'Mr. Fulton, it was a pleasure
to take care of you. There will be no charge.'"
There will be no charge

for the light or the sea's
skillful flippancies with it,
for the moon softening
the scene with its own
peculiar politeness.
After years of plea-bargaining

with a snooty muse, I've landed
here, where there's nothing I dread
doing. Gifts fall into my hands
from unindicted coconspirators; suddenly
all three Fates shine
their everloving light on me.
I'm free to watch the dunes
take on the chill
color of shells, the sea
threaten and beckon like a roof's edge,
an absentminded thing.
The way the tide rips itself
out sideways, thoughtless as a torn seam.

And people find things here I've heard:
Portuguese dolls, once encased in airy
pink and green crinolines swish in,
their mouths still
red and pouting. Here on the fragile tip
of this peninsula anything could
return. I'm half-prepared
for hostile mermaids, pilot whales, stranded
miscreants clad in moss and furs.
I'm half-prepared to see my father
to whom the world gave nothing
without struggle, rise up beaming
anyway upon it, as if he never meant
to let it go. Saltboxes appear and disappear

in the slurry fog. Gulls open
against the sky like books
with blank, beautifully demanding pages,
and behind me the stolid ocean
slams itself on earth
as if to say *that's final*
though it isn't. Behind me the ocean

stares down the clouds, the little last remaining
light, as if to remind me of the nothing
I will always have
to fall back on.

POWERS OF
CONGRESS

1986-1989

Shy One

Because faith creates its verification
and reaching you will be no harder than believing
in a planet's caul of plasma,
or interacting with a comet
in its perihelion passage, no harder
than considering what sparking of the vacuum, cosmological
impromptu flung me here, a paraphrase, perhaps,
for some denser, more difficult being,
a subsidiary instance, easier to grasp
than the span I foreshadow, of which I am a variable,
my stance is passional toward the universe and you.

Because faith in facts can help create those facts,
the way electrons exist only when they're measured,
or shy people stand alone at parties,
attract no one, then go home to feel more shy,
I begin by supposing our attrition's no quicker
than a star's, that like electrons
vanishing on one side
of a wall and appearing on the other
without leaving any holes or being
somewhere in between, the soul's decoupling
is an oscillation so inward nothing outward
as the eye can see it.
The childhood catechisms all had heaven,
an excitation of mist.
Grown, I thought a vacancy awaited me.
Now I find myself discarding and enlarging
both these views, an infidel of amplitude.

Because truths we don't suspect have a hard time
making themselves felt, as when thirteen species
of whiptail lizards composed entirely of females

stay undiscovered due to bias
against such things existing,
we have to meet the universe halfway.
Nothing will unfold for us unless we move toward what
looks to us like nothing: faith is a cascade.
The sky's high solid is anything
but, the sun going under hasn't
budged, and if death divests the self
it's the sole event in nature
that's exactly what it seems.

Because believing a thing's true
can bring about that truth,
and you might be the shy one, lizard or electron,
known only through advances
presuming your existence, let my glance be passional
toward the universe and you.

Disorder Is A Measure Of Warmth

Out of whose womb came the ice? and the hoary
frost of heaven, who hath gendered it?
                                    —JOB 38:29

In the window, frost forms cradles
                more fail-safe than the beams
        of string kids knit
                between their fingers.

Listening deeply, we might fancy
                infinitesimal clicks
        as each tailored wafer builds
                its strict array,

though the tiny silence
                of the crystal's
        like the giant quiet
                of the heavens in full swing.

No wonder hundreds
                named their daughters Krystal
        after a goblet
                of blond starlet

on TV. Madonna Paradox, she
                forges a perfection
        older than enzyme or ferment
                within the human melo-

drama of protoplasm and cell.
                The rapt nation stares

at panes that quicken
    with kidnapped infants,

love children, surrogate
        mothers. "Dynasty"
    means wives breeding
        boys to wear men's names

like designer labels
        in greedy immortalities,
    the live-forever-
        land of ads. The coiffed plots,

rote gamut of affairs,
        formulaic chablis evening
    clothes are pleasing
        as snowflakes or crystals:

ignorant things
        that succeed in being
    gorgeous without needing to be
        alive. How deeply we,

the products of chance collisions
        between wrinkled linens,
    full of eccentricity and mission,
        want to be like them.

Self-Storage

"Doesn't that feel great?"
asks Aerobia, Goddess of the Body.
Those muscular curls, ribbons of fire
beneath her skin, give good definition
to the wilderness stashed within.
She's smoothing out the kinks and nicks:
perfection is necessary in a gift.

That's why we dress our presents
in foils and tissues.
Lions lie down with lambs
across each Christmas.
There's a nice democracy to it:
each thing entices equally,
and the trim prolongs the tension
before possession
when lessening begins.
So you want a pet and get
an air conditioner.
From this, you learn to want
what you are given.

When my mother was ill and I was little
I made her a mint jelly sandwich, which she ate
or hid because it was a gift.
The misprisions!
If only we got what we deserved.
In our family, plenty lay naked
beneath the tree on Christmas.
My parents didn't see the sense in wrapping
what we'd only rush to open.
"Let's get down to brass tacks."
That was one of their expressions.

So I was surprised last summer
to receive boxes done in holly wreaths and manger
scenes from home. Thick layers of "invisible"
tape held notes—"two kitchen towels," "one nightgown,"
as if to forestall false hopes.
The only mystery was my mother's candor.
And I was mystified at Christmas
to find she'd wrapped presents
for herself, even tagging them "For Mary."

But all the gifts dropped like hints
of what the giver wants
can't change the fact
of who is giving.
Whether roses come from boss or lover's
a distinction like that
between epidermis and skin.
"Though dadgummit," pants the Goddess,
"there's a point—lift . . . three . . . two . . .
one . . . —where it gets compulsive."

And where's that? Where
buyers spend big bucks on little nothings
at the cut-rate malls?
"We cash checks," each chain implores.
Last Christmas while shopping
I stood still, watching snow
machines forge the hills
to calendar art. "Michigan Collision"
stood beside "Self-Storage":
cubes holding the dislocated
against fire or theft. Near the freeway
where cars whisked by
like sweepings, the goods
and I stood to just one side.

A child swathed in floral layers
touched my hand
at last like something up for sale.
"That's not a fake lady," her mother
said, pulling her away.

Personally, I prefer gifts too big to wrap:
the inflammatory abstracts, say—
love, forgiveness, faith—
that sear through any paper
so packaging them's like tucking
flames into tuxedos.

Maybe all presents are presumptions.
Giving, we test our affinity
with hidden wishes. Yet asking
changes both desire and deliverance,
as when lovers must say touch me
there. No matter.
Some things we'd gladly have
from any hand. Give us this day
in the pliable rain,
a solitude unlike a lidded wilderness,
a soft death—now doesn't that feel great?

I wouldn't say so. No.
What we want is another and another
day rising behind firm skylines,
a pink ridge shining into brick.
But when wasn't *always* not
less with dawn? O bright box
ripping in its own good time—

Powers Of Congress

How the lightstruck trees change sun
to flamepaths: veins, sap, stem, all
on brief loan, set to give all
their spooled, coded heat to stoves called
Resolute: wet steel die-cast
by heat themselves. Tree, beast, bug—
the world-class bit parts in this
world—flit and skid through it; the
powers of congress tax, spend, law
what lives to pure crisp form
then break forms' lock, stock, and hold
on flesh. All night couples pledge
to stay flux, the hit-run stuff
of cracked homes. Men trim their quick
lawns each weekend, trailing power
mowers. Heartslaves, you've seen them: wives
with flexed hair, hitched to bored kids,
twiddling in good living rooms,
their twin beds slept in, changed, made.

The Expense Of Spirit

The credits and debits of cold sex:
Release, power, what the back-to-basics fuck-
You on the subway adds up to.

Are we making love yet?

Look, fingers speak and shine the world. They count.
I'd think twice before bagging them
To pass for guns, or cocking
Them through the flesh of some
Likely one whose hand you wouldn't hold.
Endearments ease the deal. Which sounds callous,

Though neither she who guns her reproductive
Engine, whining "Can he be *niced?*"
Nor he who speaks of sex as "making *like*,"
Damning the heart till it rankles, playing with ashes,
Exchange the compliment I mean: to praise the otherness
Rising or widening next to one's own
Nude dilations. We care to an hygienic extent. No more, though
Earth and self get ugly when unloved. Cellulite
Skies where heaven stared! Suffer, but don't let me
See: that's the dearest, cheapest prayer.

The Fractal Lanes

Being menial, how can we let vastnesses strike through
Our fastened nerves, or see—being the ordered smallnesses
We are—the whole spill, squeeze, and boiling without
Losing heart, mind, or being
Insinuated—hugged or struck into the unwanted
Northless utmosts, the Southless balconies between
Gables of dust, rotundas of sun? Can it be our comfort's

Derived from our dumbness? It's good to know there are infinite
Exponents within the arrays we've made, that our laws block less
Visible more spectral evidence. Maybe a little
Equity—currently scarved in subterfuge—some
Linchpin—circumspect, magnetic—is yet to be
Opened and made cogent. Practice makes
Pattern. Repeat a thing till the *again*
Sculpts presence. It's some world when

The power leavening each cell's so variously
Hushed that we can't see or hear it. The thrill's in thinking it
Exists as latent prism: the red, yellow, and blue

Rays within a spun concolorous white wheel, the phrases
Interwoven down the left side of some poems, which might stay
Ghostly and unknown till pointed out. Though we base the stars'
Hermetic chemistry upon the light they hurl,
The earth's so close our measures blur. We go by lakes

And rumblings from the core. To think the ground we glide on then
Reside in holds more oxygen than the air! It makes our dying
Meager, too evident for credit—that unreckoned—breadth.

Losing It

You feel a hard-core blankness
gain the upper hand
while the world turns to glittering
silica, crinkles and rolls
up like a rented movie screen.
The air whirrs: surely
the golden fan that halos saints' heads,
electric and on high,
is rising from your spine.
Before your lips hit the floor
you recognize divestment
and want to dicker, please heaven,
with the slippage, but find yourself
dismissed. Getting lost

was once adventure. As a kid
you and a kindly aunt played at it,
boarding any bus that puffed along, no matter
where it went. Your aunt was mindful
of the transfers, which saw you home
intact. Where is she now
with her calm tokens and cerebral maps?
When your brain's become a Byzantine cathedral

flooded with the stuff of sump and dumpster.
Its frescoes—memories—confetti
into the mortal sludge.
From domes filleted and boned
with light, the impounded soul looks down.

You wake up dumb
as something fallen off a turnip truck
into a new Dark Age. That petrified

river round your legs must be your skirt.
What month? What day? the doctor asks.
Mortified, you lug the answer, a book
dense as a headstone, to your lips.
"I don't know," you whisper.

If brain were body
yours would be unmuscled
and standing in the buff.
The ooze of stupefaction
extends for blocks,
and you have nothing
but a cotton swab
with which to mop it up.
Above the bed, like a sylph
in a filmy sarong,
his head on a plate
of light, Christ sinks
into a blue plush cross.
Pain was never so fey.
Heroic, yet decorative,
he is the way
we wish death to be.
How well he embodies our need
for pleasantry. The oxygen is delicious
as champagne. You wish
to express this dim epiphany.
You'd like to
binge on the fidgety past,
but thoughts sigh slow as elevators
from cell to cell.
And words . . . words are snow
crystals to be grown from vapor.

Outside, the setting sun
dips a straw into the trees

and drinks their green.
This time you are lucky.
You've lost nothing
to speak of: a contact, a way of seeing.

Thinking back on what happened, you imagine
the brain as Byzantine cathedral, flooded
with the stuff of sump and dumpster.
Its frescoes, memories,
confetti into the mortal
sludge. From domes filleted
and boned with light, the impounded soul
looks down.

Then you discard the flood,
which was a kind of comfort; let go
the pan-religious romance of the soul.
What's left—a state
that's strictly ex- and un-,
not-this, not-that, the ne
plus ultra of losing
track: a nothing so engulfing
I had to hide behind
the second person to address it,
as though I spoke of someone

else. I remember my mother
folding my aunt's best blue pajamas
on the empty drawer of her
dresser in intensive care.
If there's a soul it's such
a clingy rayon casing,
deflating almost to absence
when creased in layers of tissue.
From the high ground of health
and self-control, I issued orders to

Try. Her lids, pinned by ether,
strained as she complied.
Squeezing a hand I hadn't
held since childhood, I wanted to forget
myself and beg her to awaken.
Come home, no matter
where you're headed,
the voice inside me said.

Silencer

When snow soothes the view, it doesn't pay to reason
with each shapely flake of its sinless topsoil.
Better admire the crystal's moronic tolerance.
Better call the proud happy,
the past fixed and finished lives
convicted parts of history.
To live is to be a threshold that persists.

The mind wants to rest its reasons
against the framed snowstorm it keeps inside
the living room, caged in Zenith or something Japanese.
It wants to meditate upon the marrowless Zen
ecstasy that froths between the channels,
to think the moon's the sort of thing
toward which the earth is tending: over.
Over and out. The mind thinks people

die because they have no reason to live or die
for their reason for living since a reason for
living is also a good reason for dying. Then the living
invent more reasonable deaths since the suicides' invention
might be catching. The reason for life might
be to make us want to leave. When friends advise

the mouth to consume more cruciferous vegetables,
the mind to swaddle itself in thermal
thinking, rent a screwball movie,
Pillowtalk, all winter,
the mind thinks something impolite.

Once a force called *she* exists
it can't be made to de-exist.
Though the centuries spend as stuff

before the ongoing (in which nothing's gone
for good) happens to snap cells into something
singular and capable of saying "I"
might be *forever* squared. Welcome
to the blitz indifferent and long-

lived as grit. What a lottery win
it is to live. She was a channel through which
energy traveled in a way it won't again.
But the mind's sugar labyrinths insist
there is a soul: think surround sound
from hidden speakers, think air-
grams, weightless blue. The mind thinks
when death usurps my turbulence that lightening or loss
goes up in soul. It thinks if only.
Then builds tough stuccos of no, ending with no
matter how it waits she won't return.

In the meantime there are common flickers
on the lawn, words to whittle, friends to kid.
In the meantime minds pose and put
each other on with drastic poise.
And though the sun is lustrous
on the snow, minds want to switch on
every watt inside. They want to rest their every
reason against the gusts of blank repose
within their sets and make their blizzard babies.

The Pivotal Kingdom

A head capsized the wild mechanism of May
and a body followed, casting off
its muddy husk.
I gazed at him from the raised walkway
of the excavation site,
through dust the color of suntan.
I wanted to stroke a thing so warmly
smooth, a uniform khaki, on bended knee.
I wouldn't mind touching hands
tensed round centuries
of hiatus in place of vanished weapons.
His motions tabled for millenniums,
he'd had a long word with the earth.
He'd lodged in its plutonic gut,
an emptiness strung with pulse. Like all mortals,

I have a nodding acquaintance
with the dark.
You know our slogan: Keep it light.
The tiled tunnels beneath rivers, fallout
shelters, the undersides of bridges
where sunbeams slither
like lizards on adhesive toes
are good at holding
shadows. But shadows aren't hard
blackness as much as patterns
made by lesser light.
Even our refrigerators are stuffed
with glow, like well-appointed homes.
Though it's no strain to visit the abandoned
mines beneath Detroit,
the transformers choked in power

lines under Manhattan's tailored granite,
I wouldn't want to lodge

in the clay warrior's dense bed.
I'd miss the inner city
of sensation so solid you'd swear it was
embodied: yearning, an expansive
mansion in the marrow; pain,
a charger of barbed wire;
and joy, a freed slave hoisting
hallelujahs through the nerves.
But is this private sector hidden
in heart or brain or bone?
Does it hold
eminent domain inside our heads, live in
vivid ampules under wraps
of fat, swim through tissue's minnowed shadings,
the opalescent flecks of cellulite
like spectral residues
in flesh? As Socrates said
life's intrinsic
to the soul but accidental
to the body. He said
if the spirit does exist
it isn't a good mixer. In my book
inclusions are not accidents,

though accidents exist.
It's best to conscript them,
the way jazz repeats a slip
till it sounds right.
Just think, it was a mistake
made by plants that created oxygen
and led to us, builders
of plants that change air back

to what our lungs can't trust.
The pivotal kingdom holds

crossbows rigged against intruders,
terra-cotta soldiers guarding
rivers reproduced in small,
and shuttlecocking constellations
at the top. Walking, we're borne
up by glancing blows
that form the ground, spirit cities
fraught with once and future
euphorias, with wars.

Trophies

Over stiff blossoms of cocktails, firm studs of leathered dens,
bucks give perpetuity
above-it-all glass stares.
Their nailed heads must rest secure
their sum lives on the other side
of plaques they wear like pillories.
How wise, how benign they seem.
In contrast to the spiked heads of deposed
dictators, the hors d'oeuvres of history.

Don't trophies mean golden droves of loving cups
incumbent upon glass? Or keepsakes
that preen like sculpted flak,
tureens full of blackout saying the kick in the groin,
the bayonet hung with guts are here made clean.
A tone higher than the note
broadcast by merchants to kill vermin
holds their alloyed atoms intact.
They will last longer than your children,

those vases for bouquets of zilch and zap.
No rosebuds rise like screwed-up lipsticks
from their brass tubes. Brass wombs
they bear transcendence
without blood, pus, piss, spit, snot, or come.
Like children, they cry I won, I won!

Cherry Bombs

At five I knew at twelve
the body's logic
would lead to blood, rah-rah

girly pom-poms, breasts, the secondary sex
signs shaved to lady-
likeness, arrayed in labial

pleats for the world's ease, a skirt
on an escalating gender:
the flatness developed in steps,

a corequake certain
to insinuate me up
despite my fast dissent.

I hated the world's complicitous *give
in, give in.*
Though the shot

silk slips, Lilt perms, and Ambush
scent seemed lusciously adult
a suspicion lingered they were lures

to an unfixable forever
I deeply didn't want.
What did training bras train

breasts to do?
Hadn't I been told
when strangers offered dirty candy

to say no? I said no
to unselective service:
First comes love, then comes marriage,

then comes wifey with a baby carriage!
Prams pulled girls to ga-ga conversations
while boys made GI Joe advances

loving the loud sounds of their mouths.
At the beach I saw
the fate they called "expecting."

Labor was a squeeze and scream
we couldn't play at
making glamorous, like war.

I wanted no part of that combat, no
thank you, no
compulsory unsung heroics, please.

Please immunity. Please a dispensation.
Mother, are there monuments for women
dead of children?

Child, women are the designated weepers
at monuments for men.
But no one engraved spirits

behind the tiny engraved names.
We grew toward an undoing
punctual as mutual.

Boys put on ugliness young:
Filigreed cap pistols
swiveled them to targets,

pulled red strips and banged
on dots of dust
until the air smelled warm

as baking day but different.
Boys trailed their guns like magnets
drawn to polar charms.

Guns swirled like weather vanes
with boys instead of cocks above.
They dropped each other

into herohood, expecting
the chance of bullets
in their flesh, the mold

under their nails, the mold
of uniforms. They saved face
daily, scraping themselves free

of down and drowning
in Vitalis. They turned their hearts
to cherry bombs.

Of age and corseted
in shells, off they went
into the Aqua Velva yonder.

It wasn't that I wanted to be not
female. I wanted to be female
as I was. When another frilly being asked

"Do you have the pretty kind?"
I understood her
meaning: We loved our no-count

cunts and vulvas, though we lacked the words
till high school's titters,
its biology nuns all nuts

and bolts.
"It's what's up front that counts"
sloganed the voice-

over selling filtered smokes.
At five I thought the secret
of eternal life was simple

as keep breathing: Out/in.
Girl/boy. Truth/lies.
No one could make me

null and void.
"Would you rather be liquidated
or boiled in oil?"

my sister's witch voice
drifted from the basement.
I thought about it

the rest of childhood, all day.

Our Calling

To birth shape from the spill

                To silence *is to kill*

To raise Cain from the matrix

               Dislodge   disperse   dispatch—

lifting thoughts from nil

            the clean words for murder

It's our conspiracy to see

           Overlord's *a lord supreme*

the world one way

        and code name for the Allied

empire by which we pledge

             invasion,

allegiance every time we speak

         of Northwest Europe   A battle tactic

a narrow anthem by which we zero in

           is called an Operation

What's disarticulate doesn't exist

         after the knife   the blood

Nothing wakes in our head

       that makes us well

unworded   The unnamed   stateless

         in clean surrounds

sink into the winter page

       we call the theater

unless we carve a clause of granite

         High drama's the standard!

build snug

     Weapons etc.

canons or grand rescue

        are ordnance *from arranging   making neat*

At best   it's plenty

     The enemy? Never

Its penultimate horizon says
                    let them choose their names
no zenith   no matter
                    Christen them Blemish   Vegetative
how we reach
                    Gook   Kraut   Cunt   Zip   Slit
At worst lies pit the mother tongue
                    Gossip stands for tales
as salt on roads
                    of birth   epic
dry-rots the goddess
                    songs of war   in short
The world waits for our orders
                    To man *is to make*
It haunts
          active   To woman?   *Fill in*
our heads   the atomized
                    the blank
fuzz of gnats
                    Those icons finding whys
barely there
                    for war we call
visible only from uncertain
                    memorials
personal slants
                    The preferences of men
except that from the swarm
                    we call our culture   *Our end?*
we forge our terms
                    Will beings known as us know all—
except
          inclusive death? Oh yes
we call each shot
          We call it loss of personnel.

Trouble In Mind

A murdered body's shallow grave.
A ditch that shelters sniper fire.
Who says memory's a friend? Who'd grieve
to find their sleep unrifled, furred

by a select amnesia? Because I thought
recalling all turned all to sense,
I filed my life in pieces, all that
debris changed to meaning, all scenes to signs.

As soldiers dismember weapons to check
on their perfection, I broke the said
and done. Blame's the bullet you catch
between your teeth or worse, inside.

And if some angel dust or peace
pill, busy bee or killer weed
could turn the past to has-been, a poison
shot let bygones be, who wouldn't

try it? The stuff of Agent Orange,
which says the world's no matter, gutting
every ghost within its range.
A jungle of nothing. A forgetting.

Hardware

I don't know how this silk-screened memory
expansion board—its soldered subdivisions
exposed yet unembarrassed as a city seen from air—
holds a million bytes that flame
to words when touched, but it does.

It sits on my desk like a skull
or a phone, another sculpted composure.
I like a phone because I can hold it
and join the circumference
of radial cables that bind
the earth's hot core with voice.
And I know a touch that sends it
on a global search to snare the line
I need, immediately.
Technology is something

to rely on when your clothes catch fire,
as mine did all last year.
I don't know how the everyday selvage
from my closet became a conflagration,
but what a spectacle I made
in my candescent dress!
Trying to run from what consumed me
only urged it on.

When my friend said, "Hold still,
I'll help you out," I was distracted
by a hundred molten buttons.
Wrapped in that emphatic shift,
I lacked self-discipline.
Besides, even a fiery daywear covers
nakedness. Only love can disembarrass one

to strip. When I did
I kept undressing
long after all the clothes were gone.
My skin felt like brimstone,
so I thought I'd take it off.

I don't know if the comforts of others—
the man who visits fabric stores to play
with bolts of silk that ask for nothing
when he's estranged,
the woman who test-drives cars
she'll never buy to feel
the annointed engine fire—
apply to those who don't know how to live or die.

Still, my friend has given me a memory
expansion board of turquoise pools
and resilient springs,
a thing outside myself to hold
whatever sharp endowments
I choose. And I choose the trees

harboring little pneumatic drills
outside my window, trees infested
with the fricative fuss of small soft birds
along Le Forge. "Le Forge Road—
Isn't that where people go
to dump old stoves?" a man asked at a party.
Yes, and where they come for frication
in the front seats of foreign cars,
their drunken consonance
riding on the wind to me.

I don't know if drivers in those lively confines—
where windows rise electrically,
wipers wave at misplaced knees,

and rear defrosters sap the battery—
find ease, a soft exchange
that's more than fabrication, but I like to think
they might: those drivers who remove their synthetic
permanent press suits
to remove their suits of fire.

For In Them The Void Becomes Eloquent

Dusting under nuptial covers,
the virgin working for the matron
wondered what love had been. A light
housekeeper, she tried different accents. Sixteen.
She stressed the light
in her job title, made believe
she was in charge of bits that drill the dark
for those at sea. A *light*house keeper, she.

The virgin borrowed her mother's vacuum, that was how
she got the job. How she made the windows quiver

like drops about to fall.
Ammonia smelled mean
but left no streaks. It grieved her to think
bright banisters continued
while humans would be dead in seconds.
Once she'd worked for a Home: the old stowed away
their mashed potatoes in the dresser drawers.

God was infinitely excellent,
thus sin was infinitely bad, the Little Sisters said.

The forever fire was precisely right
as punishment, being eternal
but no longer than eternal.
God couldn't lose for winning, she observed.
In Him the void became eloquent, a sound

without knowledge, too high to be heard.
The vacuum's beige fury burned the dust.

It swelled like a male thing:
sooty grouse or lizard. Boys wearing autopsied light
shows for clothes were her firm favorites.
She'd work two hours for four dollars
to buy their latest, play and play it
till she had the lyrics
written in her hand.

One day light would scalpel into grooves
and make a cleaner music.

She'd discover new foods—Gruyere cheese, whole wheat—
learn to say "quiche," obtain a Visa
and be gone to stay.
Ammonia smelled mean but left no streaks.
Her mother thought this was beneath her.
Yet her mother's vacuum was what she needed
to turn down

the dark like nuptial covers,
to vivisect the night with her bare hands.

Cusp

Sometimes when night turns me transparent
I want to lie on the dispassionate ground
and make of earth a gurney
till dawn lets me be opaque.

Knowing indifference is earth's
common constituent, I can take comfort
in a coldness innocent of aim,
expecting no finesse and no affection, sink
all clamor in the caulking
that's our planet, a little weather-
stripping against space,
and be glad for density,

which lets one substance hold its place
to the exclusion of another:
the pen stay separate from the hand,
the body independent of the earth,
the skin allow no ingress,
and jail and lighthouse
fail to occupy the same terrain.

So the wings big enough to lift us
are too big for us to move!

So the soul's not stashed inside the skull
like a daffodil spring-loaded in a bulb!

Should I be grateful I escaped
pernicious heavens
when acceding to the empty
forms of affirmation might be better
than embracing disbelief?

Give me a minute while I think it through.

No cause for despair. Clinging to a planet
spinning twenty miles a second round the sun
with fourteen pounds of atmosphere
stuck to every mortal inch
and winds of ether streaming through
each cell, how could we not be well?

To the North, the Great Lakes are lit
by towers held to rocks with iron rods.
The glass hives in their heads
breed chips of glow to swarms
that slice night's infinite regress.
In winter, swags and valences of snow
turn the railings cosy as a curtained home.

By sight alone I'd never know
that ice is cold. How can I see
a cloud's less distant than a star
unless the cloud should intervene
between the star and me?

        We recognize what's closest by its power
        to obscure what's far.

Some loveliness is porous as the hush
between notes that makes up music,
the waves of hue that strum the eye,
sensations that chime
through recessed nerves, leaving
the surface undisturbed
as air allows a beacon, flash-
light or light-
house to part the dark on either side.
But only our solid abundance lets us touch.

Electrons make way for a caress.

They want our bodies to be roomy
and float through each other, forgetting,
if forces ever knew or could forget,
that the particles in flesh are dense.
The more we press the more our substance
tries to dodge duress and finds it can't,
which comes across as touch.
How odd that the body's deep resistance
lets us feel another's presence,
and our presence is bestowed
by means of protest too.

That sensation is a failed escapement!

And touch won't prove congruency:
if certain nerves are spooked
we'll feel stroked though we're alone.
Still, no harm supposing
light massages prairies with appeasement
since it neither rips nor pushes them away,
that the swishing blank expanse
of snow comes down to dust ruffles
and each knapsack of quanta
in the atom knows its role.

"I," the erogenous cusp
of mind and world, sees the rose
lining of a bird's beak
and calls the dawn a churchly blue.

But I need lessons in deportment.

How, at three A.M., to find the silo
by its denser cylinder on dark,

refract the husk until it grows
in deeper contrast to the night
and night becomes a positive
beside that lighthouse without light.

Behavioral Geography

The constancy of rainbows—or gypsum,
the 19th century's "petrified mist"—
some trick of light or distance,
made me think Niagara Falls
gentle as a crinoline and slim
enough to ford.
Statistics enforced discipline.

They say the first explorers charted all
they hoped to find: tranquil breezes, courteous seas,
beauties equaled by impossibility.
Only a wonder country, love,
could meet such expectations.
And miracles are no criteria
for the everyday.

Mercator, equator,
what's the use!
Our analytical engines go full-tilt
to make the world
look one way to us all,
Euclid freed
of every flaw.

We think reason works
best when left unchecked
by ecstasy.
So a tree beglamored by autumn
sun seen in the blemished rays
of history turns out to be
the hanging tree.

I wanted to define here, there,
and get back home intact. Believing maps
blocked access to influential realms,
I sat an inch from you,
saying, "Who goes there?"
awkward in the face
of all I didn't know and must

suppose. I filled in the blanks
with dragons, found hobgoblins
in the stop and go.
And you became pervasive,
a wandering monument to every major
nonevent. So zero
raises the value of a sum times ten.

I cling to wishful visions
like someone clinging to a tree, complaining
that the tree won't leave.
Hope springs up in me.
Lost, found, bewildered,
when will I learn
to like unsettling transits,

to use the universal
corrective of the sky,
a continental drift
with nothing fixed about it?
Once a woman dressed in wood
lunged down the falls,
as if her flesh were not

irreparable, and lived.
The beauty's the impossibility. Proving?
All views are seasoned

subjectivities, beds
carved by freshets,
warps of the heart.
Ecstasy has its reasons.

Art Thou The Thing I Wanted

These unprepossessing sunsets
and aluminum-sided acres
retain us like problems
more interesting than solutions,
solutions being perfect

lots of condos, the groomed weather
of elsewhere. Well, we must love
what we're given, which is why
we get stuck
on the steel-wool firmament

of home. Since it's the nearest
partition between us and what,
we choose to find it peerless.
And maybe why we wish
to lean our heads on the dense rocking

in a particular chest, as if the only
ocean lives there or a singular wind
swarms where that heart begins.
Sometimes a passing friend
becomes a mascot in our lives,

day in, day out. The thought of this anybody
affects us like a high
pollen count, inspiring a suffering
not unto death, but petty.
Having a crush is the expression.

And we do feel pushed over, compressed
by chaperones we half-asked for.
Take me, take you. Say someone quips

"Your favorite so-and-so got drunk
and said to say hello," I accept it

as a secular blessing. I glow.
Glorious things of thee are spoken!
There should be a word for you
muses of unreason, like "vector"
since vectors have magnitude

and direction without a physical presence.
And the second meaning is "carrier
of infection." Don't we resent
the way our minds circle
unfavorable terrain for easement,

like jets above imagined runways?
Yet we like to be immersed, no sweat, in solutions
cooler than 98.6 degrees,
which explains the lure of fantasy.
"You never wanted," people say accusingly,

as if glut were gladness
rather than a bargain struck.
But what comes to live here—burrs
through clay, brown negligence—
comes to live without

certain fertile perqs. High-tension
wires droop their rules
between harsh Eiffels in our yards.
Eyesores at first, they quickly become
backdrops whose presence nests

in every residence unseen.
And when a line falls, the field sizzles
for a million inches without a sign

of flinch. Yesterday the elder
out back up and tumbled.

It wasn't hit by wind or lightning,
which made the sight of it—suddenly
half hanging on the barn
like a besotted lover on an arm—
more frightening. The trunk was hollow,

devoured by some tree disease.
In a few hours the limbed fluttering
looked normal on the lawn,
and its jagged profile fit
this make-do neighborhood of farms

run in the ground by agri-biz:
The three wilted pickups
in the yard, the tire of rusty geraniums
and sign that reads Beware
of Dog where there's no dog—

the tree looked right
at home among them, metaphorically
on its knees. Like others,
I mistake whatever is
for what is natural.

You know the commonplaces. How people think
women are good
at detail work when that's the only work
they're given. Or how
the city's invisible

engines jiggled our coffee
till we believed quivering a constant
property of liquid.

Everything happens to me, I think,
as anything reminds me of you: the real estate

most local, most removed.
As on the remains of prairie
the curving earth becomes a plinth—
from which we rise, towers
of blood and ignorance.

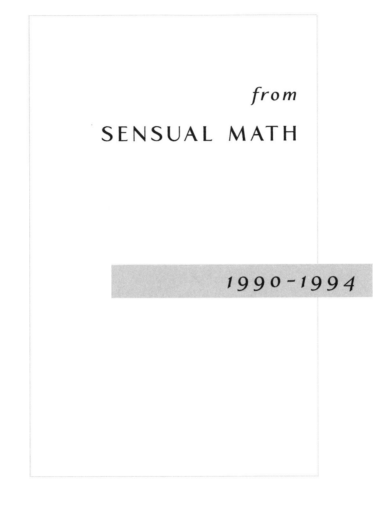

from

SENSUAL MATH

1990-1994

The Priming Is A Negligee

          between the oils and canvas. Stroke the white
sheath well into the weave. The canvas
needs more veil. The painting
               should float on skins of lead
white coating—or its oils will wither
the linen they touch, its colors gnaw
at cloth until the image hangs on air.
          The canvas needs more veil.

             The body takes its own shade
      with it everywhere. There are true gessoes
        flesh will accept: blocks and screens
to keep the sun just out of reach. Creams
      white as styrofoam but less
perpetual, vanishing like varnish
once they're crammed between the cells.
     So skin is sheltered
         by transparencies, iced
    with positive shadows. Sunshade.
The nihilist is light.
         Printers know it's the leading

between lines that lets them be
swaddled in the rag of stanzas.
How close the letters huddle
     without rubbing. For immersion see
"passion between." See
opposite of serene. For synonym and homonym
see "rapt" and "wrapped."
        There is a gown—that breathes—

and a gown—that heats. One to hold,
         one to release. Watch

the lead white camisole go up
   in arms and hair and skin.
That one flings it like a shiny jelly
   to the floor. With beautiful frugality, go
the solid cotton briefs.
   The lovers get so excited

to think—nothing comes between them.
        There is nothing between them.
That's how they can consume each other,
   sand each other sore.
The oils are suspended
   on a leading. The lovers
touch in linen walls.

About Face

Because life's too short to blush,
I keep my blood tucked in.
I won't be mortified
by what I drive or the flaccid
vivacity of my last dinner party.
I take my cue from statues posing only
in their shoulder pads of snow: all January
you can see them working on their granite tans.

That I woke at an ungainly hour,
stripped of the merchandise that clothed me,
distilled to pure suchness,
means not enough to anyone for me
to confess. I do not suffer
from the excess of taste
that spells embarrassment:
mothers who find their kids unseemly
in their condom earrings,
girls cringing to think
they could be frumpish as their mothers.
Though the late nonerotic Elvis
in his studded gut of jumpsuit
made everybody squeamish, I admit.
Rule one: the King must not elicit pity.

Was the audience afraid of being tainted
—this might rub off on me—
or were they—surrendering—
what a femme word—feeling
solicitous—glimpsing their fragility
in his reversible purples
and unwholesome goldish chains?

At least embarrassment is not an imitation.
It's intimacy for beginners,
the orgasm no one cares to fake.
I almost admire it. I almost wrote despise.

A Little Heart To Heart With The Horizon

Go figure—it's a knitting performance every day,
keeping body and clouds together,
the sky grounded. Simulcast, ecumenical
as everywhere, stay and hedge
against the bet of bouffant space,
you're the binding
commitment so worlds won't split.

Last week we had Thanksgiving.
The post–cold warriors held a summit
full of East meets West
high hopes. Why not hold a horizon?
Something on the level, equitable instead.
They said the U.S. Army held rehearsals
on monastic sand. In the desert,
lieutenants zipped in camouflage
thought back to where horizons were
an unmade bed, a nap
on the world's edge.
Privates, nights
when they were sanded
by flower fitted sheets, ground out
in flower fitted skin: her, oh him.

This Michigan is short on mountains,
long on derricks
needlenosing heaven, making evil
electromagnetic fields.
"Talks on the fringes of
the summit could eclipse
the summit itself," the anchor
admitted. Go figure.

Your reticence, your serene
lowness, because of you I have something
in common with something.
Your beauty is *do unto me* and who am I
to put you in the active voice?
I rest my case
in your repose, a balance
beam, point
blank closure
that won't—bows are too ceremonious—

close. You graduate
in lilac noise. You take off
and you last.
You draw all conclusions
and—erasure, auroral—you
come back. But I am here to vanish
after messing up the emptiness.
I am here to stand
for thanks: how it is
given, hope: how it is
raised. I am here to figure
long division—love—
how it is made.

Some Cool

Animals are the latest decorating craze.
> *This little piggie went to market.*
> *This little piggie stayed home.*
It's a matter of taste.

I have this string of pig lights for the tree.
Each hog is rendered into darlingness,
rendered in the nerve-dense rose
of lips, tongue, palm, sole. Of the inside
of the eyes and nose.
> They wear green bows.

Driving home these bitterly Michigan nights
I often pass the silver bins of pigs
en route to the packing house. Four tiers to a trailer.
A massive physical wish to live
blasts out the slits
as the intimate winter streams in.
A dumb mammal groan pours out and December pours in
freezing the vestments of their skin
to the metal sides, riddling me
with bleakness as I see it. As I see it,

it's culturally incorrect to think
of this when stringing pig lights on the tree.
It's chronic me.

> Our neighbor, who once upon a life
> hauled pigs to slaughter,
> said they are confined in little iron cribs
> from farrowing to finishing.
> Said steel yourself
> this might be unpoetical and spoke

about electric prods and hooks
pushed into every hole.
About: they cried so much he wore earplugs.

While trimming the tree, I stop to give thanks
for the gifts we've received,
beginning with *Elvis's Favorite Recipes.*
I'd like to try the red-eye gravy—
bacon drippings simmered with black coffee . . .

"Some had heart attacks. Some suffocated
from others stacked on top.
They were pressed in so tight—
hey, what kind of poetry you write? Well.
They suffered rectal prolapse, you could say."

Why not spend Christmas with Elvis?
Invite your friends
to bring their special memories of the King.
Put a country ham in the oven and some of his songs—
White Christmas to Blue—

About: somehow a pig got loose. A sow
fuzzed with white like a soybean's husk.
It was August and she found some cool
under the truck. When he gave her a Fig Newton
her nose was delicacy itself,
ticklish as a lettuce pushed whole into his hand.

Are You Hungry Tonight?
I speak from the country of abundance
curdled brightly in the dark,
where my ethics are squishy as anyone's, I bet.
I'd like to buy the enchanted eggnog fantasies.
Instead I'm rigging the tree with grim epiphanies
and thinking myself sad.

For a gut level of comfort,
close your eyes, smell the pork chops frying,
put on "Big Boss Man" and imagine
the King will be coming any minute.

"At the packing house, some bucked like ponies
when they saw the sun. Some fainted
and lay there grunting to breathe.
Drivers hooked the downers to the winch
and tried to pull them through a squeeze.
Their legs and shoulders tore right off.
You'd see them lying around.
After the showers, they turned a hysterical
raw rose. They shone. The place seemed lit
by two natural lights, coming from the sky and hogs.

Pigs are so emotional. They look at the man
who'll stun them, the man
who'll hang them upside down in chains.
They smell extinction and try to climb
the chute's sides as it moves.
At the top, the captive bolt guy
puts electrodes on their heads
and sends a current through.
I've heard the shock could paralyze
but leave them conscious, hanging
by their hocks from the conveyor
until their throats are slit.
Pigs have an exquisite will to live."

After eight months he quit
and got a job screwing tops on bottles
of Absorbine, Jr.

Now when people ask what kind of poetry I write
I say the poetry of cultural incorrectness—
out of step and—does that help?

I use my head
voice and my chest voice.
I forget voice
and think syntax, trying to add
so many tones to words that words
become a world all by themselves.
I forget syntax
and put some street in it. I write

for the born-again infidels
whose skepticism begins at the soles
of the feet and climbs the body,
nerve by nerve. Sometimes I quote
"At mealtime, come thou hither,
and eat of the bread,
and dip thy morsel in the vinegar."
Sometimes I compose a moaning section,
if only for the pigs.
Like surgeons entering the thoracic cavity—right,
the heart's hot den—
I've heard we could slip
our hands into the sun's corona
and never feel a thing.

Echo Location

Stop quivering
while I insert straws in your nostrils
and wrap your head in cloth
I have immersed in plaster.
For a life mask, the subject
must be rubbed with gelatin.
And you must be the love du jour.
I have studied the duct-taped mullions
of monarch wings for inspiration.
I've learned the paramedic's rip.
Don't squirm.
(But I ran my finger down its spine
when its back was turned.)

A perfect containment invites trespass,
the wish to shave below the skin
and write in seed ink, *mine.*

I can testify
the tic of prayer persists in nonbelievers.
Under my distressed surface, under duct tape,
the Hail Mary has a will of its own.
The spirit uses me. It holds me up
to the light like a slide.
It claims a little give, a quiver,
can prevent a quake.
Says copy the vibrato inside trees—
the star shakes, heart shakes—
that ruin the wood commercially.
Says you must be ready

to freeze your extremities
anytime for a better glimpse of the blur.

Not the blur made firm, mind.
        The blur itself
and not a clearer version of the blur.
        Will you hold it up to the light like a slide?
        Will you pledge your troth
                        and tear this edge off first?

The Norman name for quiver-grass
was *langue de femme.* As in gossip, as in meadows,
        one ripple leads to the next, as in cascade
experiments: one touch and worlds take place.

That's why a little quiver can inscribe a night
                into your left breast,
a day into your right. Can shave below the skin,
                and write in seed ink, *thine.*

But when I think I've ripped the surface
                to the pith, queen substance,
        when I've diagrammed the cry, I

        remember a quiver is a fist
of arrows and the arrows' case, their clothes.
                        Is the weapon and the tremor,
                the cause and the effect.
Once the arrow leaves the bow—
                        will-of-its-own-will-of-its-own—
there is no turning back.
        You must be the visceral river.
You must think a little give
        leads to affinities: the arrow
                        resembles the bird it will fly into.

two poems from **My Last TV Campaign:** A Sequence

THE PROFIT IN THE SELL

You know that existential twilight
found in rooms lit only by TV?
How the consuming starlight
grinding from the screen will pass
for dusk no matter what
the hour? I ask you. The sun never sets
on "Dynasty." And somewhere
you can bet "Bonanza"'s always
inflicting its tempestuous Western fairy tale
on the air. *Broadcasting.*
It means to throw seeds.

I had retired to find myself
considering the ads I'd written
flashing through every private-
public space in declamatory cascades.
Supplyside, right
brain stuff. IVs to the id and ego.
Get it said and sold with style
in 30 seconds, you get loud fame. A Clio!
High honors for the catchy cobwebs
you sewed in someone's head.
Before being tucked into oblivion,
I wanted to raise something more
than mercenary monuments
to high sales curves.
I'd rather be emerging than retiring. I came out

to sell a big account
that needs to keep its identity

hidden. They're deep
into everything it seems.
A job so sweet you'd do it
for free. Career candy.
I couldn't wish away the rush I felt
once I grasped what they were after:
A campaign that demonstrated the beauty of dissolving
boundaries between yourself and the Martian
at the heart of every war.
An ad that pushed viewers to incorporate-embrace
rather than debase-slash-erase the other
gal-slash-guy. A commercial saying blend,
bend, and blur, folks. It works!
But how to put this spin on their opinion?
How to position—this position?
Advocacy ads are not for beginners.

I was struck by a case history
that was no *once upon a time*.
It really happened, the Discovery
Network said, over some vast stretch.
This orchid fashioned itself
into a female bee, or you
could say, a commercial
for that creature.
By dressing up and passing
as a dummy luscious *she*,
the bee orchid pulled in more
pollinators and survived more

flagrantly. So what, you say. *So what?* So
it was evident. The deep shape of everything is—
transvestism. I know
it's a difficult sell.
Mimicry's a prettier word.

Creation is a form of crossdressing. The ultimate
one-size-fits-all. When he heard, my partner put on

his man-of-the-world-
weary look. "Orchids in drag? Don't make me
laugh." He was ready to throw hooks.
I was ready to throw odes
in the path of flowers
brave enough to reach
beyond their typecasting and accede
to victory. Poets. Or killers.
Good copywriters are either.
If you're both, you get rich.
I wanted to commit sonnets

in honor of these—maximal outsider—carnal flowers
that overstepped their bounds
to complete themselves
with bees. "Complete?" Wilderness
and wing—incessant escalator—dice and fathom
in the stems, the spine's
expansive gossip and
the prophet in the cell—

emerging—coming out,
dispensing with what's stable is what
it's all about. Art, nature, name it,
are fresh recombinations.
My ode goes "Imitation, soul
of innovation! Memory's naught
but summer reruns, reflections
of the sun inverted in the sea." It goes and goes.
As nature knows, it's easier to mix
single-celled existing things
into new and improved blooms

than to build the blossoms straight
from protoplasmic scratch.

When the orchid special ended, I surfed
the channels of hypersmiling families,
steamy crops of frozen foods,
drop-dead erotic cars.
But if television's the common—
village square and looking glass
held up to the big US,
why did I feel sunk
inside the cranial guts
of a machine that made the whole thing up
according to its whim?
I watched that sucker thinking: Its power

is its costume. Its costume
is its *signal*, a trait that changes difference
to affinity. I poked the remote
till my arm felt carbonated, full of Coke,
thinking with the ads
I'd sent thrashing
through their electronic cottages
how I'd inflamed the nation
to spend. I got out my charge
to analyze the charm of its design.
It's the size of holy cards
from childhood, the word
DISCOVER dulled
by the membrane of my prints. The logo's

letters simulate a dawn
or dusk of commerce or wonder—gaining
on the world. What else
to expect from flesh and sense? What rises

more gracefully
to the mercantile occasion or better sets
the earth at rest? Sentenced
to the breakthrough and
dispersal of the day,
the sun does
time and promises. They've made it
the white navel—I notice—in the O.

from **My Last TV Campaign:** A Sequence

*You asked me what my flowers said—then they were
disobedient—I gave them messages.*
                    —EMILY DICKINSON, LETTER 187

What eucharist of air and bland

was this nation raised on? No one understood
my funny flowers—and Darwin—

Darwin was regarded as a charlatan.
Few viewers think

evolution is the truth.
My flowers *were* absurd.

Snips of sugar. Snails with spice.
Puppy dogs. Tales. Everything.

Nice!

But why did I admire nature so?
Was it that I liked

the absence of a Master
neuron in the brain—

the absence of a Master
cell in embryos—

the nothing in the way of
center that would hold?

What causes less comfort
than wonder?

What—does not console?

==

It might mean immersion, that sign
     I've used as title, the sign I call a bride
after the recessive threads in lace ==
the stitches forming deferential
        space around the firm design.
          It's the unconsidered

mortar between the silo's bricks == never admired
        when we admire
the holdfast of the tiles (their copper of a robin's
     breast abstracted into flat).

     It's a seam made to show,
the deckle edge == constructivist touch.
     The double equal that's nowhere to be found
        in math. The dash
     to the second power == dash to the max.

It might make visible the acoustic signals
of things about to flame. It might

         let thermal expansion be syntactical. Let it
add stretch

        while staying reticent, unspoken
as a comma. Don't get angry == protest == but a
comma seems so natural, you don't see it
when you read: it's gone to pure
transparency. Yes but.
        The natural is what

poetry contests. Why else the line == why stanza == why
     meter and the rest. Like wheels on snow

that leave a wake == that tread in white
without dilapidating
mystery == hinging
one phrase to the next == the brides.

Thus wed == the sentence cannot tell
whether it will end or melt or give

way to the fabulous == the snow that is
the mortar between winter's bricks == the wick that is

the white between the ink

Fuzzy Feelings

Is beige a castrate of copper, pink, and taste?
Does lace add blush to any situation?
Do you want novocaine?

I've been staring at the ceiling's
stucco moonstuff for three hours, grateful
for the prickly little star
someone's inked onto a lattice strip.
This light means business, like a xerox

of the sky's allover glow.
I'm seeing nonexistent rainbows
outside, transparency split
into the true colors it hides behind
its see-through guise.

Is the universe an imitation?
Are the cat's tabby cables
a mimicry of snake? How can you tell
a natural emerald from the flux-grown fakes?

Inside it's all beige
partitions, latex gloves, lace tiebacks
and prints of ducks in love.
The drilling decor and rock
make me think I'm in a bodyshop
through which a boudoir's wandered.

Metaphor is pure immersion. Pure sinking
one into another and the more
difference that's dissolved the more ==

often I'll sink
into a book that swimless way.
Some volumes turn out to be wallpaper
or boxes for valuables. Simulants

tend to be flawless, while natural
emeralds have defects
known as inclusions, imperfections
with a value all their own.

I'm faking Lamaze and ancient mantras. I'm having
new veneers. The dentist talks about a relative
who boasted over 364 girlfriends
and seduction rooms in every shade.
He was in air conditioning
and smoked himself to death
though he could hold his breath
longer than anyone else.
"My role model," the dentist says.

Do women need fuzzy feelings?
a man asked in the waiting room's
frayed *Glamour.* Do they need simulated intrigue
dinners, candlehours, cuddle-wuddle
teddy bears and wittle tittie tats?
Anything with ribbons on it,
an earthtone rainbow baby angel goose and floral bed.
Do women need texture and men
need sex? "To stick it through
the uprights," this guy said.

Scientists think the universe was smooth before it loomed
itself to a jacquard
of defects known as textures.

A texture is not localized.
It's an overall sensation, like being

enthralled or born, in love or mourning, growing
at the speed of light and leaving
its distinctive signoff on
the sky. Photons—lumps of glow—
gain energy by falling into
a texture after it unwinds.

"I hate rock," the dentist says,
changing the tape for its clone.
What does beige == what does lace ==
what does pain imitate? The autopsy
of beige revealed a gelded rainbow,
upwardly mobile ideals. Lace
is a form of filth I hate.
As for the dying moan and gush

of the deer killed by hunters down the road—
I'd find it more tasteful
done in plastic or an acrylic
venison Christmas sweater.
I'd rather wear vinyl than hide.

I didn't mean what I said about lace.
Lace in a vacuum would be okay.
Even beige would have its place. It's context,
culture makes them == wait, I'll take the novocaine.

When I get home, I'll fall into the immense rub
of a robe like a universe unwinding.
I'll talk to Sandy
whose daughter Laura died last year.
(I hate the type's authority in that line, the—
get it in writing.)

When a friend asked how Sand was doing
her husband said "She'll never be the same."
"What a relief it was—to never have to be
the same. I felt so grateful," she explains.
The return to a genuine, originary self
was—thanks very much—not to be

expected. Her imitation would see her through
another evening of held breath.
As we left the "slumber room"
she asked whom Laura most resembled.
I think she == you, I said
in some wrong tense.

Before a party, she blends some body
veil into herself. Gets ready to flex
the verbal abs and delts and hopes
she won't be up till dawn
re-living how she broke into
emotion during her free pose.

Does "grace" mean alive and lucky
to be not writhing?
Or the ability to hide it
when you writhe?
The fissures == vacancies inside

a natural emerald are known as its *jardin*.
I'll leave this place with a refined smile
outside a headache that makes me cry all night.
Right now I'm trying to open wide.

Southbound In A Northbound Lane

A fetish is a story masquerading as an object.
                    —ROBERT STOLLER

Her anatomically correct smile
turned to frown when she turned
upside down: the inflatable naked woman
the student body tossed, cum laude,
through the graduating bleachers.
Like gossip, a bubble bred for turbulence,
                    she tumbled
to the Ph.D.s, who stuffed her
under their seats.
            I think the trick to falling is never landing
            in the palm of someone's hand.
The lyric, which majored in ascent,
is free now to labor and cascade.
What goes up must = =
                    Waterfalling
means the story visits tributaries
at a distance from itself. Consider
what it takes to get us off
the ground: what engines laying waste
to oil. I'd rather hit the silk
from a span
and let gravity enhance my flight.
Though the aerodynamics of jets are steadystate
and can be calibrated,
I'd rather trust a parachute,
            which exists in flux and can't be touched
by mathematical fixations.
            In what disguise will she arrive—
            whose dissent is imminent yet unscripted—

offensive as necessary?
Whose correct context is the sky.
Arrive like something spit out of a prism
in a primary tiger bodice. Be modern
as an electronic vigil light, precisely
delicate as nylon,
the ripstop kind, that withstands
40 pounds of pull per inch.
Spectators, if we jump together,
we'll bring the bleachers down.
"I was frightened. My flesh hissed
and I thought I'd perished,
but the sensation of descent vanishes
once the body stops accelerating.
It's astonishing how nothingness
firms up. Air takes on mass.
The transparent turns substantial.
I stretched out on that dense blue bed
until the canopy expanded
like a lung shoved from my body,
plucking me off the nothing matt.
What held me up was hard to glimpse
but intimate as mind or soul.
I sensed it was intensely friendly.
I almost thought it cared for me."
If you can't love me, let me down gently.
If you can't love me, don't touch me.
If we descend together
like Olympic skydivers or snowflakes
we can form patterns in freefall.
Like a beeswarm, we can make a brain
outside the body.
When falling is a means of flying,
the technique is to release.
How many worlds do you want,
my unpopular bodhisattva?

Let's sneak one past the culture's
fearless goalies, be neither one
nor the other, but a third
being, formerly thought *de trop.*
Before I throw my body off, my enemy
of the state, I'm going to kneel
and face the harsh music
that is space.

Immersion

Let it be horizon levitating on horizon
with sunrise at the center ==
the double equal that means more
than equal to == within.

It's sensual math
and untied railroad tracks ==
the ladder of gaps and lace
unlatched. It's staples
in the page and the swimmer's liquid lane.
Those sutures that dissolve into the self.

      Once by night she shoved blunt needles
      through the cotton sheafs. Once.
      By God for the nth time. She'd give
      her stitches extra hiddenness.

Pile dash on dash and stroke the seam-
ripper down the middle.
Let a blank fall down
the posit that never disappears.
If you love the opposite of knot,
the way the center point in shadows can be hot,
let it do what it wants ==
to grade the white space like a passing
lane to passing strange.

      By night she burned and dodged
      to polish up the image.
      She agitated paper in three poisonous solutions
      until a picture formed.

It's the partly present == that leads the view
out of the frame onto the wall
and lets you finish
the dismembered thing yourself.

      Though her day job named bureaucracy
      the one infinity
      she'd get before she'd get to heaven,
      by night she learned a tongue by thinking
      only in that tongue. She worked her mind into
      its language like the tines of a glove.

So one thought is occluded by another
no less celestial mention in your head ==
each sinks in each
as paper can fold back onto itself.
When you unpleat, the crease lingers
and each wing wants to press == consensual == into
the other once again.

      By night she sank jewels in immersion cells
      to understand them better.
      It is a test: when gem and liquid share one
      refractive index, a continuum
      exists and the solid's limits seem
      to vanish. She tried solutions till the stone looked most
      completely gone. When there was least gem left,
      she could identify it.

Yet immersion's also treason
to a naming that's a nailing down.
It's the barcode riddled down the middle
so the product's up for grabs ==
what no register can scan.

I use it like a comb to unsnarl day
and sift the blank
in tones in hopes
the prism will begin
its tints in me. Which is to say.
I'd be close to you as glass is to its double
glaze and music to its stellar disc.
I'd be all give. Let me put it like this ==

five poems from **Give:** A Sequence Reimagining
Daphne & Apollo

THE LINES ARE WOUND ON WOODEN BOBBINS,
FORMERLY BONES

A daughter like the openwork of lace == between
                the raised motif

              the field, formed by lines
    of thread called brides, shies back

      in order to let shine. The design
            from negative space

      shapes its figured river == suns
star == the white thorns == sperm == and patterns

verb the ground. Through the brides'
           or pearl-ties'

airy flesh of net, wayward electrons
           spin

      with their absent grace and
           windowing

      through the opaque == the dense
      omissions crystallize the lack

      that's lace. She is to be that
           yin of linen

that dissolves
under vision's dominion == be the ground

of silk that's burned away with lye ==
the bride.

from **Give**: A Sequence Reimagining Daphne & Apollo

UNDOING

Take:
her wish to be chaste. And exist in violent cloister.
To be unravished as a prime
of rainbow—a red or blue
unsplittable
through any prism. Take
the as-it-is-as-it-is—
the script. Use two hands and twist.

If you're a virgin, what are you doing
running around the woods, getting raped?
Curving every which way
in nonconjugal space.
Don't you know the best manners are the least
obtrusive? Your presence pursues its own undoing.
Just asking for it: Just use two hands and twist.
As it is as it is: your femaleness naturally
says take. Says this rape has your name on it.
Your beauty provokes
its own dominion, whose no can never mean no.
How does that one go? TO OPEN
SCRIPT PUSH DOWN WHILE TURNING

While spinning her negative charge
she has—like a wave—no single location.
If pushed through a slot, her velocity
compounds. Take
a hue outside the spectrum,
an unchromatic octave
higher than the eye can see,

a singular—unravished shade. Name it she.
Her color, name it nevergreen.

As to her bareness and her glance,
he wants to array it in flame
sandals and flame veil, a white tunic
with a double-knotted sash.
Give it an iron ring.
Put on its high-heeled sneakers—put
its wig-hat on its head. Its dress
of a fine smooth textile
made in filament and staple form
from wood pulp
solutions extruded through
spinnerets
and solidified in baths or air.

He wants to part her hair with a lance.
To make her rayon likeness,
evergreen as glance. His composite
new improved her. Cast her
in fibers of modified wood pulp found in
butcher linen or tire cords.

Prestige involves accumulation.
His desire to collect her
assumes a type—and others of the.
A kind—not one of a.
A whole forest to be had.
Let arrows stand for probabilities.

If he bored in close he'd find her bare
charge higher than it seemed == an infinite
beneath an infinite shield == an infinite
that can't be split
by modifying in the middle.

Neither soft nor hard, dull nor
bright, she traveled fast and had no given.
The more he tied her down as to position
the less he knew of her
momentum. Always transported, always elsewhere
before he == *who was she*

to tabernacle in the woods?
Place a minus sign in front of it.
Haze her
escape. TO OPEN——LINE UP ARROW
ON SCRIPT AND VICTIM
PUSH SCRIPT UP WITH THUMB.

No matter how many of her he gathered together
in his name, she would not
be the natural he could cultivate.
Though cast as lady or grotesque,
as hectic membrane in the flesh,
she would be neither-nor.

SUPERNAL

Apollo pulls a cloud back like a foreskin
        on the sky that is his body.
His laserscope will amplify
        the available starlight,
zero in on the nymph
      in her stealth boots
        that leave no helpful scent.
Daphne—who is graphite,
      darkling, carbon as the crow—

             is out of breath.
If only the stars would tire,
      she might find cover.
If only they would empathize.
      But who will help a person
      on the wrong side of a god?
All largo, she turns to face Apollo.

Though she expected him
        to wear blaze orange, supernal
as the sun, he tracked her down in camo-
      skin, which "disappears in a wide variety of terrains."
He owns every pattern in the catalogue.
       After considering *Hollywood Treestand*
          ("all a nymph sees is limbs")
       and *Universal Bark*

          ("a look most guys relate to")
       he chose a suit of *Laurel Ghost*,
       printed with a 3-D photo of the forest,

which "makes you so invisible
only the oaks will know you're there."
Even his arrow's shaft is camo.
Only his ammo jackets gleam
like lipstick tubes.

Is it any wonder, when his wheel-bow
has been torture-tested
to a million flexes,
his capsicum fogger
fires clouds that can cause blindness,
his subminiature heat detector
finds the game by the game's own radiation,
and the tiny boom mike in his ear
lets him hear a nymph's grunt from 200 yards—

any wonder—when the ad said
"Put this baby to your eye
and see if she's worth harvesting" and
"See the hairs on a nymph's ass,
up close and personal"—
that he turns the housing, gets her
on the zeroing grid,
and now his snout at her fair loins doth snatch?

Who can she turn to, the monastic, almost
abstract Daphne?
The stars are tireless. She decides—
no, winds up—
pleading, in extremis, with her father:
". . . I am not like
them, indefatigable, but if you are a god you will
not discriminate against me. Yet—if you may fulfill
none but prayers dressed
as gifts in return for your gifts—disregard the request."

That's when her father makes her
                into nature, the famous green novation.
And Daphne—who was hunter and electron—
                is done with aspiration.
Did you see it coming? You're a better man than she.
                With no one to turn to—
                she turns to a tree.

TURN: A VERSION

(*Tree*)

She'll get out of this one somehow. Someday she'll break
our engagement
with a wraparound roll-off or axel full twist
dismount,
followed by a blast of wind that puts an end to this
grotesque togetherness.
"The suckers love a weird wedding." That's what
her father said when
she called on him for help. Forget Io and Arachne. He was
thinking Teenage Mutant
Ninja Turtles. Roger Rabbit, Mr. Ed. People get a kick
out of ambivalent
betrothals and collisions full of give. Flowers that
remodel
themselves to look like bees are nice, but the scientist whose
atoms get commingled
with a fly's might be my favorite. "Help me! Help me!"
I can identify.

Yes, it tamed her, being changed into a tree, but consider
what went
on in me. I had a moment's prodrome, the premonition
before seizure or disease.
I heard voices—"Hi, I'll be your server for tonight" and
"Can I see your ID?"
Then in a migraine pink epiphany, I knew I was
a tree. "It"
turned to "me." As Daphne sank, ensorcelled by my thorazine

hush, I heard the
whitewater rush of what I was. To you it might have seemed
"the tree heaved upwards
and twisted like a sleeper in brown sheets" but the process
felt plaid
to me, like madras bleeding—color stabbing color

as it never does
in nature. Heavenly hurt. I recognized the presence
of design.
She moved through my zen nap like a queen—
yes Your Deviance—
riding up like a skirt, abrading my chambers and rays till she
crowned. Oh,
she was a sensation. It was not consensual, let me tell you.
Whose "no"
can never mean "no"? I was opened and she was spiralbound
as nature/culture,
the great divide, broke down. "I'd like you to meet Daphne,"

said the River God, her father.
Please—what's the word for opposite of—"like to meet
Daphne"?
What's the word for what is doing ground loops, flying
the great circle course,
uppity, aspiring, reaching 100 knots in me?
Daphne apparently
did not know her position. I experienced tremendous
interference.
She said she was changing to nighttime frequency: it was dark
as a casket where
she was headed. "What is your position?" I transmitted.
"Partly cloudy,"
she responded. "What is your position?" I asked again.
"Approximate.
Whistling now. Please take bearing on us and report . . ."

"We are unable . . .
it is impractical to take a bearing on your voice," I said.
"We are circling . . .
must be on you but cannot see you," she came through. I felt
the lead tickle of her

ribbons, her heavy mittens with a trigger finger stitched in,
her nuclear skirts and
coppertoed fauve boots. She was carrying an old Kentucky
rifle, a Pioneer
Drift Indicator and a "very orange kite."
"I'm dead meat,"
she said, and then—"I am not friendly." That must be when
I freaked. I drooled
amber as trees do when they're hurt. I salivated
resin blond
as baby shampoo, lactated the bud-gold of
extra-virgin
olive oil to trap the pathogen, Daphne, in a gown of sap
for good.
What's the phrase that means how fast the growth layers
spin? Velocity of
domain. I circled her in no time, head to toe, in a million
wedding rings.

My first emotion happened to be revulsion: an ungreen, sour
cramp
as Daphne shrank—"oh baby," he kept saying—from
Apollo's colonizing kiss.
Of course, he liked her better as a tree. "Girls *are* trees"
was his belief. Mediated
forms pleased him. "If you can't find a partner, use
a wooden chair,"
he'd say. Well, every fetish tells a story. I felt her bows
and powders,
guns and arrows change to pom-poms, a cheerleader's pleated

skirt.

"As she jumps up try to pull her to the sky and slightly
forward," he coached.

"Every beat in a yell should have a motion. Give us an A,
Give

us a P! End the yell with a good freeze." Then her power
mount pike

through—she tried to get away—became
a shoulder straddle

to cradle—as "Nice Save!"—I caught her in her grave.
I choked

on volts of hairspray as—step-step-step-ball-
change—

she became his pep club. Pure as a
symbol,

toned, in racing trim, for her just standing still was grim.
"Safe

in your alabaster chambers," she'd sigh. I noticed she became
more babyish

as the centuries passed by. She couldn't walk, had no control
over her body,

and often babbled rather than talked: "Sis-boom-bah. Doobie-
doobie-doo.

Oo boy or oo girl?" Frivolous. Gerber's gibberish.
And I

became her pacifier. She called me Mr. Crib.

Oblique
grain develops after an injury—like Daphne
teething

on my rings. The growth tornadoes, polarity
breaks

and the grain departs from the ideal of straight == deviating ==
making waves

that form diverse and beautiful chambers. People find it

hard
to say which way a tree is spiraling—whether dextral or
sinistral—
and mistakes are often made. The Germans say with or
against the sun,

the English, clockwise or counter, from the on-high
perspective of the gods.
In America, the vortex is described by observers
on the ground, with much
twisting of wrists and waving of arms. But no one sees it
from the standpoint
of a tree. Oblique grain is useless for transmission
poles, plywood, or veneers,
and so a tree with it is thought abnormal: a "monstrositat."
But spirality
isn't a sickness or condition. Since it makes me less desirable
to commerce
and being harvested is not in my best interests, I consider it
a plus.

I had zero spiral before Daphne. I've heard the aberration
depends
on what it turns against. And every part of me has turned
against
a woman's body. The stretchmarks *she* developed are a story
in themselves.
We talked by thought which made us really close.
Others
might consider her a kvetch, but we became best friends.
I understood
because I *was* her by then, wrapped up in the electric flex
of her
ideas: I learned women were debarred from sweating and
vision seeking,
that the female was the prey of the species . . . adapted

to the egg's needs
rather than her own. When Daphne first heard this she'd
begged her father,
saying "Feed me, also, River God,
lest by diminished vitality and abated
vigilance, I become food for crocodiles—for that quicksand
of gluttony, which is legion. It is there—close at hand—
     on either side
          of me." He agreed but later, of course, he changed

her to a tree. To me
she was unnatural. People don't realize—"natural"
is a habit.
Once otherness gets in, a something else entirely begins.
Newness
isn't truth so much as emotion. At first, I resented her
efforts
to transcend me. It was like sleeping with a jostled beehive
in my stem, between her
vengeful "next times" and torrential "should-have-dones."

I said
"You should have sought your *mother's* help when trying to
escape."
But face it, mothers were the ones who bound their
daughters'
feet. The experts said deflate him with a spike heel or a hat
pin, but
who wears such things? Not *this* wood nymph. And he was
a god,
for Christ's sake! He had all the stellar leverage. He was a
tactician
of infinity—a god! Her mother, Gaea, was the Earth Goddess,
yes—
but she'd always pressured Daphne to major in Home Ec.
"Man produces, woman

reproduces." Her mother took that line. "Why can't you
be a gatherer
like all the other girls?" "Next time I'll go for the less

embedded delicacies," Daphne cried. "I'll mime 'little'
with my index
finger and thumb." I'll say this: she wasn't a pleaser.
She lacked
a slave mentality, though she modeled herself on Apollo's
twin and "modeled"
is probably too weak a word. She *did* Phoebe. She had a
Phoebe act.
It was Phoebe this and Phoebe that. She ran with Phoebe's
band and cut
quite a figure as The Little Sureshot Riverbrat, Maid of the
Myth, with a star
on her hat. She could snuff a burning candle with a bullet,
break
five eggs before they hit the ground and pierce the ace
of hearts.
All with her back to the target, while aiming in her compact.

When captured,
she kept shooting through my cambium, reaching beyond
the bodycast
of lassos I'd become, and her hand, part of her hand, her
trigger finger
I think, got slammed outside my trunk and is preserved there
in amber, an organic gem.
If brass were clear, it would resemble amber. If wood were.
Silk as flesh
kept always clothed, gold as cologne, as beer, as urine, warm
to the touch,
absorbent, *elektron* in Greek or substance of the sun, light
in the fist,

amber—collects a negative charge when rubbed. It preserves organic tissue
very well, which might explain why Chopin handled
amber chains
before performing and Roman soldiers wore amber-studded
mail
as their palladium. I was surprised to find 200 terms for it
in certain
Polish dialects. But no word exists that is the opposite of
"like to meet Daphne."
The more private the wish the less likely there's a
term
for it. Did I say she's always having visions, as in ancient
versions
of the myth? She sees herself discovered, maybe

in my side,
washed out of context, or buried in blue earth. She'll tell
her story
rather than be held inside its web. There are holes—
have you noticed—
where the seams don't quite close? Daphne peers through
those gaps. She
scans the sky and plans to stare—you can almost hear her
glance—
down the air, the blank, the optical until
a face stares back.

A NEW RELEASE

(*Daphne*)

A voice changed to a vinyl disc, a black larynx,
spun
on the hi-fi as we called it, before light was used to
amplify
and the laser's little wand got rid of hiss. The
diamond-tipped
stylus stroked the spiral groove and guitars flared out of
reticence:
the first bars of a hit. I always wanted to hear it
again,
though it was always in my head: sticky,
invasive,
and what else in that culture was that
dark?

Easing the new release from its sleeve, I saw myself
bent
out of shape in its reflections: a night whirlpool or a
geisha's
sleek chignon, an obsidian never reached by skin
since skin
always has a warmth of blood beneath. It was a synthetic
Goodyear black,
like all records, pressed with a tread the needle traced,
threading
sound through ear and nerves and marrow. I touched its

subtle
grain sometimes wondering how music lurked in negative
space
that looked so unassuming. The marvel was—the missing
had volition.
And the spaces between tracks were a still profounder
black: darker than bitter-
sweet Nestlés, coffee ground from chicory, or Coke. Black
as it must be inside

a tree. "Wear My Ring Around Your Neck," the latest
hoodlum Cupid sang.
He aimed at objects and hit people, it was rumored.
His urgent nonsense—
about hound dogs, rabbits, class and lies—changed
aren't to *ain't*,
were to *was, anything* to *nothing.* "Caught" was the operative
verb.
While couples jived and twisted I must have listened
differently—
as to a special pressing—with my head
against
the set. Somehow, by the last chill tingle of the cymbal
I wanted
to be the singer rather than the wearer of the ring.
To this day,
rodents gnawing at the wooden walls remind me of the rasp

of dust
before a cut. A cut. That's what we called a song.
And handsaws—
harvesting the forest in the distance where I live—
sound
like the end: the rhythmic scribble of stylus against

label
when everybody's left. Everybody's gone
to bed.
And the record turns and turns into
the night.

from

FELT

1995-2000

Close
(Joan Mitchell's *White Territory*)

To take it farther would mean dismantling doorframes,
so they unpacked the painting's cool chromatics
where it stood, shrouded in gray tarpaulin
near a stairwell in a space so tight
I couldn't get away from it.
I could see only parts of the whole,
I was so close.

I was almost in the painting,
a yin-driven, frost-driven thing
of mineral tints
in the museum's vinegar light.
To get any distance, the canvas or I
would have to fall down the stairs
or dissolve through a wall.
It put me in mind of winter,

a yin-driven enigma and thought
made frost. When I doused the fluorescents
it only became brighter.
The background spoke up
in bitter lungs of bruise and eucharist.
Of subspectrum—
a sentence left unfinished because
everyone knows what's meant.

It was a home for those who don't go out
for sports: the closeted, oddball, marginal
artists in the storage of the world's indifference,
whatever winters await us next.
I was almost in its reticence

of night window and dry ice, its meadow
lyric barbed in gold, almost

in the gem residence
where oils bristle into facets
seen only in the original, invisible in
the plate or slide
since a painting is not an illustration
but a levitation dense
as mind. As this minute
inheriting its history along innumerable lines.

== The enigma is so diligent ==
I miss it when I visit it ==

It shrinks to *winsome* in a book.
Its surface flattens to sleek.
In person, it looked a little dirty.
I could see the artist's hairs
in the pigment—traces of her
head or dog or brush.

== I stood too close == I saw too much ==

I tried to take the long view
but there was no room.
I saw how turpentine had lifted the skin,
leaving a ring, how the wet was kept
on the trajectories, the gooey gobs of
process painted in. Saw dripping

made fixed and nerves and
varicosities visible.
I saw she used a bit of knife
and left some gesso showing through,
a home for lessness that—

think of anorexia—
is a form of excess.

While painting, she could get no farther away
than arm's length.
While seeing parts of the whole,
she let the indigenous breathe
and leave a note.
She dismantled ground and figure
till the fathoms were ambiguous—
a sentence left unfinished
because everyone knows what's meant,
which only happens between friends.
The lack of that empathy embitters,
let me tell me.

== I miss you when I visit you _ _
I stand too close == I see too much ==

You put me in mind of winter where I live,
a winter so big I'll have to dismantle myself
to admit it: the always winter
and its consolations of flint.
This is not an illustration.
It's what I saw when the airbag opened,
slamming me with whiteness like the other side.
I came to consciousness on braced arms,
pushing my face from the floor
in order to breathe,
an arm's length from unbeing, as it seems.
I was what flashed through me

in full frost. We were life to life,
in our flesh envelopes,
insubstantial, air to air and you and I.
Though we could see only parts of the whole,

we felt its tropism.
We leaned toward, liked,
its bitter lungs. We almost were that
winter tissue and cranial-colored paint.
We were almost in the picture. We were close.
We left each other a note.

Fair Use

As for the sofa, its fabric is vermiculite,
glittering, as is trans-
ferment. My head's already in its sixties flip,
Kennedy's already dead. Incandescence
has a heavy hand. For all I care,
the TV might be an airshaft

> when the statics of *is* widen and show everyone
> meshed, a fabric of entanglement ==
> my consciousness felted with yours,
> although I didn't know you then.

> It is not metaphorical, the giver is
> literal beyond prediction about this:
> what happens to others happens to me.
> What joy, what sad. As felt

is formed by pressing
fibers till they can't be wrenched apart,
nothing is separate, the entire planet
being an unexpected example.
Is this fair use, to find

> the intergown of difference
> severing self from == nonself == gone.
> I grasp the magnetism between
> flesh and flesh. Between
> inanimates: the turntable's liking for vinyl,
> the eraser's yen for chalk,
> the ink's attraction to the nib.

> What lowercase god sent this
> == immersion ==

to test my radiance threshold?
From then till never == time, space, gravity
felted to a single entity,

though the backlash of epiphany wasn't all epiphany's
cracked up to be. Synthesis is blistering.
I've often wanted to get rid of ==
it. I couldn't get rid of it. It

resists wear and as it wears, it stays
unchanged. There is no size
limitation. It
expands equally in all directions as more

fibers are pressed in. No matter how stripped
of cushion, needlefelted one
becomes there's no unknowing what

can be compressed a thousandfold
undamaged, won't ravel, requires no
sewing or scrim. What is

absorbent, unharmed by saturation.
What draws and holds, wicks, that is,
many times its weight in oils or ink.

Listen, I didn't want your tears in my eyes.
I wanted to keep my distance, put a silence
cloth == ironic == lining == frigid == interfelt ==
between us. My
students == teachers == parents == sisters ==
get your hearts out of mine,

I wanted to say. It can be hard
enough to drill or carve or turn
on a lathe. It can be sculpted.

It dyes well. The colors lock. At times
I've prayed that the unfrayable gods who gave it
would give it to a rock.

Maidenhead

In the closet, the dress lives, a deep white in its vinyl
bag, its crepe ivoried, tartared
like a tooth, feeding on what leaks through
the zipper's fervent mesh, an unmentionable,
unworn, waiting, immortally in mind. Open

a window, please, I'm feeling faint. On the bus home
from school, I'm reading Dickinson, living on her

aptitude for inwardness and godlessness, thinking
of the terror she could tell to none
that almost split her mind.
She made solitude honorable. But how hard
it would be to keep ink off a white dress
or keep black cake crumbs or lily pollen off,

how difficult to have only one dress and that one
white. Unlikely really, likely

to be a myth. But don't tell me that at seventeen.
I wear the same harsh uniform each day.
Narrow choices seem natural, strictures
more common than their opposite,
and I am always famished, crushed
on the bottom stair, the door closing
its rubber lips on my hair, trapping
lengths of it outside—

Last one in is an old maid. Your aunt is
mental, some kid says. There is a lace

of nerves, I've learned, a nest of lobe and limbic
tissue around the hippocampus, which on magnetic resonance
imaging resembles a negative of moth.
She felt a funeral in her brain. Somehow I get the fear
of living in the world's unlove forever
better than I get the cheerleaders' braced grins.
I understand my aunt's mind as the opposite of
Dickinson's, though Dickinson also was unnormal, her white
matter more sparkingly aware.

You understand the dress in stanza one is mine,
my one white dress, in which I'll never

shine at graduation, in whose chaste V
the nuns won't stuff linty lumps of Kleenex
to keep covertness whole. In winter in upstate
New York, the snow is too bright on the bus window,
too crusted with singular crystals that toss
sun around inside them the way diamonds pitch
the light between their facets,

gloss to gloss. My aunt lived alone, as you do,
and if that sounds presumptuous, I meant it

in the sense that your head is mostly cloistered
though symptoms of your innerness leak out.
You know, the blush of a pink diamond
is caused by structural strain.
But her aloneness was deeper, I think,
than your own. Hers extended miles below
the surface, down, deep down
into pleats where no interfering rays
can reach and thought is not veiled

so much as sealed. A cap of lead.
Not veiled

since a veil's a mediatrix, at least in the West,
negotiating sun and glance. Veils screen
a virginal reserve == the mind, I mean, or maidenhead,
a crimp at the threshold, figured as door ajar or slip
knot now, once thought to be homogenous,
a membrane nervous and dispersed
throughout the body, more human than female,
both linkage and severance, the heart and brain
sheathed in its film of flesh and pearled
palladium effect. It is the year the nuns change

their habits at Catholic High, while the senior girls
spend recess studying *Modern Bride*, learning

how Honiton == a bone lace
favored for Victorian veils == was rolled
rather than folded for storage, sprinkled
with magnesia to remove the oily substance
which gathered after contact with the hair,
cleaned by being covered
with muslin and the muslin lathered
and rubbed until the lace below was soaked,
at which time it was rinsed, dried betwixt

the folds of a towel and sunned
for twelve hours till it looked new

and had no smell. If anything has no smell, it's a gem
and gems are seldom, the rare results
of deviance beneath earth's skin, of
flukey stresses that get carbon to exalt into
the flicker of a pre-engagement ring, a baby diamond,
as solid and as spectral as
a long white dress flaunted by a
girl with nothing else. There's an optical effect,
interference, I think it's called, that puts the best

light on a gem's flaws, transhimmering
its fissures into vivid == Your flaws
are the best part of you, Marianne Moore wrote,
the best of me too, though as I write it, I recognize
an obvious misquote. Stet and stet again,

place dots under material marked for deletion
and let it stay, let the starved crystal raise

its hackles across the gap inside the gem ==
the trapped drop become a liquid momento,
let wave trains of light collide
from aberrations and give the thing a spooky glow.
Prove—like a Pearl. The paranormal glow

or "orient" of pearls exists between
the nacre shingles, and nacre begins, as is

well known, with injury, a dirt that must be
slathered with the same emollient
used to line the inside of the shell. Solitude deepens,
quickening, whether hidden or exposed as those girls
sunbathing by the gym at noon in the thick of winter,

Janelle, the only black girl in the school,
who covers the white album with foil

and buries her face in the blinding book it makes
so that, as she explains, her skin might reach
the shiny jet of certain Niger tribes
or the saturated blue-black of subdural bleeding.
Her transistor, meanwhile, plays a blues that goes

I got a soundproof room, baby, all you got to say is
you'll be mine. I visited

Dickinson's white dress in Amherst where
it stood in her room, looking so alive it might be
but for the missing head. The phantom pains,
escaping diagnosis, led to bolts of shock—
and tines of shudder—volting through
her mind, my aunt's, that is—stricken into

strange, her language out of scale to what
she must have felt, and Dickinson's metaphors—

And then a Plank in Reason broke—no help.
The doors are locked
to her little house, she has removed
the knobs, leaving deflorations you can peek through
once your eyes adjust, up the stairs and to the left

beyond the thresholds' velvet ropes you'll glimpse
the shell pink walls and hope chest full of failed

trousseau beside the single bed.
Look in upon that sunburst clock, the china creature
on a leash, some pearls unstrung, convulsions of—
the Frigidaire and oilcloth and radiator's
blistered pleats, the slot in which
we slip our fare—

"I sweat blood over this," the dressmaker sighs
at the final fitting, and I can believe it,

the pattern—imported, the seams—so deep,
the stitches—so uncatholic and so—
made for me. *Snap out of it*
someone says as we gain traction and wind
parts my hair, parts the comfort drops

my lenses float on, and I lean against
the door, the white lines vanishing
beneath us == the measure rolling on the floor ==

About Music For Bone And Membrane
Instrument ==

chords unfurling in arpeggio, that fragrance
we called Storm the Stage, Fan, Eventail, Ogi, This Girl

Who Collected All Things Japanese.
How she got me into it. Into all-night sessions
that made us late for school.
We'd paint the leaf, the paper part, then fold
the tissue back onto itself
in anticipation of a moment that came down
to open == close. To this girl
who used bitchin wicked boss or tough
as praise saying isn't it
ek-*skwiz*-it
stroking the thing with her tone, wanting me
to agree, no, not agree, feel
what she felt, succumb to her taste her
fatuation—beautifully pierced, outlined with gilt
—and I'd run

one finger down that
interrupted nocturne, the crevice between
sharps, touching substrates and binding sites that
dilate into color and design. Into extremity

pink folds and pleats,
handheld compressions, corrogations of
recluse, release.
That arc, that parabola, that phoenix and the o-
varies. That obsession that
makes the world
smell like the inside of your nose.

• ♦ •

In the 18th century, the fan had a language:

Running Your Fingers through the Ribs, I wish to speak
Hiding the Sunlight, You are ugly
Opening and Closing, You are cruel
Dropping the Fan, We will be friends
Leaning Close to Admire, I like you
Placing the Fan Behind the Head with Finger Extended, Goodbye

♦ ♦ ♦

The handling of the fan is difficult.

It's a short leap between collecting and becoming.
Fall on your knees
while they perform their musical procedures. O hear

the mortals singing. Tear the lungs from your body
while standing on a folding chair.
While they do some musical violence to your life.

The fan is made to whirl or spin to look like wheels.

Grab the binoculars. Close enough to see their crowns.
Their long incisors. Grab a press
pass to the labyrinth behind the curtain

calls, to close brushes with the creases
in their throats, instruments fretted with pearl
pick guards acrylic bodies catgut strings guytrash.

The singers produce their fans and lay them

before them, taking them up whenever they wish
to speak. For the greatest artists,
the fan and the hand are one,

though the dark areas omit detail from
material brought to light. "Are you decent?"
the roadie yelled before we = =

because she'd won the contest and requested the backside
of their necks. The spine's highest
chakra. So small

a compass may be compensation. Come
grayish briney harsh and salty
when she really wanted some sweetcream something

else. Wanted to be other
people. Wanted say Arpege. The lungs torn out
and smoothed would cover a stadium

though what a lot of pressing
that would take. There are substantial losses
in this delicate flatwork.

They often use two fans, repeating each trick

of twisting and turning with the right or left
hand, the fan being an extension
of the arm, the arm an extension of
the song. And when they finish,

the fan is thrown, spread open, backwards over the shoulder

to an attendent who catches it mid-flight. Guytrash
is English dialect for a specter
in the form of an animal. Sometimes she said

the fan is tossed so as to turn over and come

back to the hand. And this girl bit one
there while snapping shut.

        •   •   •

A gash will turn to gush. Isn't it exquisite?
I can live with it. With

a wig made of pubic hair, a one-inch capture of
a
slept-on sheet, fab skins gathered from
a
French page, a lifesize portrait executed
in
bodily fluids, puncture jewelry, tongue studs,
a
fragment of apparelling, a letter mutilated by eraser burns
and
pencil smut. I can love with it.
With
secret enthusiasm, the paper is forced into this shape

        •   •   •

much as Kafka thought
the world had precipitated
into Felice Bauer. He collected her

gestures because destiny
hides in the trivial,
and to extract the vast from the little

is a gift, like perfect pitch.
He turned her photos every which way
but she still looked elsewhere

with almost supernatural ease. That is,
if you saw a brick wall looking thus
you'd be highly surprised. Some

considered Starseyes full of Sadnesssome
felt
Starseyes light up & glisten with golden Granulesor
turn
pensive or Forbiddingsome
saw
Starseyes imbued with now a mild now a corrosive Ironysome
perceived
in Starseyes surprise and a strange Cunningsome
loving
Star pursuing star's enigma thought that Starknew
something
of which nonstars knew Nothingsome
found
Starseyes impenetrable Andsome
finally
believed that a stony calm a mortal Voidafunereal
estrange-
ment dominated Starsgazesome-

one wrote of Kafka's eyes.

♦ ♦ ♦

Higginson called Dickinson his
cracked poetess. A crack is a nasty, dangerous thing
to have around the house ==

any bolt or dovetail is
less efficient than a knot or splice ==
I find I need more veil, she wrote.
Her mind was a wire too fine to see
by ordinary means. So she persuaded
birds to perch ==
lashings, sewings, and binding are more efficient
than metal fastenings or glue ==
birds after birds, until the wire floated more
noticeably.
It expands waves flutters is raised or lowered
closes. She wrote her eyes
were like the sherry that the guest leaves
in the glass. Float of the peephole, slit float.
The picture on the leaf retains
its creases even when open.
The leaf retains
its picture even when shut.

     • • •

I still have the clothes I was wearing:
the very jeans and retro satin blouse.
The style rose

from the ovary with a maiden
hope and happiness before unknown.
The very see-thru sandals

have been lost. They gave good surface
and they gave good depth.
And when they sang their fans' multi-flap

anatomy with mobile shutters began to
imagine itself right down their open mouths
into their organ meats and things.

Insect-small they looked
through the binoculars and sodium
vapor glow. Like bees they gyrated to speak

and kept time in the dark.
Some wanted to rend their bodies and
blazon the parts—hair, nails, etceteras—

in private and in small.
One wanted a shirt pick contact
filling sock gum or butt.

One wanted a catalogue raisonné.
One studied ways of etching
dislocations using acid brews

that accept no substitute.
To fan is to starve. This girl lived on the clippings,
adding horsehair and stiffening

till they felted and became a cushion
for a single hammer in her
piano.

    • • •

Felt is often a small or hidden part
of a familiar == and thus
escapes attention. Plus one

can never hope to see things smaller
than the wavelength of the light
used to reveal them. This girl recalled the details

of Kabuki plays. Like finding it hard
to carry water, he fills his mouth and forces

the liquid between her lips.
Or pulling up his circular net
he finds a ghost in its folds.
I need French silk. This one

was talking about chocolate cream pie, but she
sounded threatening. A heavy
woman with little severed ears around her neck,
from which a miniature music, a big sound compressed
to fit the tiny sieves, cheeped forth.

Float of the peephole. Slit open float.

First I used rubber but that did not satisfy.

It was intractable, an obstacle
that could not be wrapped, boxed, or prevented

from extending to forever.

          .   .   .

The god fan unfurls to phoenix, an unbirdly bird
whose molecular sensitivity is such
that when it is about to die, it pours
from its lacerated beak exquisite
shards that bloodcurdle listeners yet

is remembered only for the ashes
from which it manages to soar seemingly
without effort, a nonce projectile
whose alliance with the everduring proves stronger
than the tenets and godtricks of physics,
this girl said.

          .   .   .

For years, this composer was paid to be the fan
      No well-dressed man or woman should be without one
of those who wanted to write music. Composer
was their guilty ID.
      Enthusiasm, an ethereal medium
      transmits knowledge
      in the manner of a contagion, a finished excitation
      you can't sleep off or cauterize.
She couldn't get her mind around it.
She was paid not to write music

but to inspire others to write it,
to adore their work as if she'd given birth to it
since nothing less could ever draw it forth.
And she did love. And she did good

sometimes, as she did fan. She tried to give
self-lubricating frames. She had sayings:
The Notes Are Forced Into This Shape and
Comfort Him Or He'll Spray.

She was dying to write, but she hardly had time
to bathe, let alone compose
works with a fragility that outlasts human life.

      This fan is quite dirty. Much worn
      on the outer sticks. There are some splits
      and thin spots. And the color

therapist poured a flask of red
stuff in the tub. She'd never seen such
a vehement soak. As if someone had slit
herself the long way, wrist to elbow,
which can't be fixed, therein.
      A gash will turn to gush.

Sometimes her students taught her a new word.
"This is a sucky scherzo," they'd say.
From the verb "to suck," which
in the last decade of the 20th century
meant a thing was trash. "My bad," they'd say.
Sometimes they made her laugh.

·   ·   ·

In the 20th century, the fan had a language.
It
ran, hid, opened, closed. Dropped, leaned, admired, extended,
said
I was gonna exchange the same carbon monoxide kind of
thing.
We nicked some leaves from Star's tree. Star saw my Big Star
Doll
while I was waiting to greet the limo. I got a dry mouth just
drinking
Star in. We went to the studio and just stood soaking. Then
it
happened. Star turned round and Star made
eye
contact and said Hi to which I found myself saying
Hello.
Wow. We were floating. Star said Oh HEAVY
fans.
My mind was so focused on Star that the edges
blurred
and I didn't click. Then Star went all SPIRITUAL
and
started chanting. Then Star threw me
the
candy from Star's pocket and motioned for me to eat
it.
That's when everyone crowded close and yelled "DON'T EAT

IT!"
I knew I could die now and go. Star knew I needed
something.
Oh I don't know how but I know how
it
feels. More than the kiss in a way as this was
so
personal. Tho it probably wasn't. Tho it did show
Star
was thinking of me as a person. And I for
one.
Star looked right at me with Star's intense
blue
eyes. Then my brain goes all wet. I was totally lost in Star's
beauty.
Star looked long, loose, and very shiny. Getting into a
Porsche
911 Targa sports car. It was Blood
Orange
in color. So I ATE it and Star smiled. Star was so nice and
Star
was so THERE. And Star wasn't ON at all. Star seemed like a
regular
person I'll never forget. Then Star threw me
the
same rose I had thrown to Star. I'd watched Star carry
it
and when Star threw it to me I was. Because Star. It was so
special
in my freezer twenty years later. And instead of
having
we both ended up crying in our beds. And I swear to this
day.

      •   •   •

That one is still trying to rhyme orange with Porsche.
When loyal and royal would be perfect.

That piano swathed in tarpaulin before a concert?
With clumps of sound trapped in its skin?

Its legs remind me of a racehorse.
Such delicate spindles beneath a heavy chassis.

And a single atom seen through
a field emission microscope resembles

a sheep in a fog on a dark evening. Guytrash.
The smallest thing one can see is a good deal

affected by the light. Scholars know
the ardent love of perfection in work

which in olden times seemed not too dearly
attained by spending the best part

of a life on a single project inconceivably small
by normal standards: tarnish collected

from the subject's cutlery, a study of
the muscle that pulls the testicles

close in times of stress, a rubbing or frottage of
an estranged music the fair finish of

which can only be appreciated
through a magnifying glass. Catch

      • • •

and she tossed me an object

fresh from the acid bath, numinous,
with a purse-like sphincter of circular
pleats, with patina in its grooves and signs
of use: pitted, pocked, etched, dented,
experimented upon. Silken from touch.
An organic polymer perhaps, which comes

expensive, or a material essentially made
from sugar rings joined without folding
whose density was similar to flax
though its strength was four times that
and virtually immune to rot.
Suffice it to say the whole affair varied

in weight and size being a hard
but cushy ball or disc with
an erectile sheen. A maybe crystal
grown from vapor? A once filament
till tiers of new grew down? A nice bubble
in the palm of my bad? In Monastral

Fast Blue, that synthetic pigment used
on innumerable front doors whose atoms
are cousin to platinum. Weight for weight
I'd have to say the stiffness was not quite
as good but it was not so very much
worse and the stuff may well prove something
developed by a private enterprise, the fibers of which

when enlarged show striped and scratched and fuzzy gray
bands running on the bias
into a vast number of layers, sleeve after sleeve & each

perfectly in place till in truth
I could not tell what it was or was
for, only from the way this girl saw it that it was

not nothing, that it had a pointedness, an intelligent
smell about it, like a veil made of birds or maidenhead
or an ostracized muscle that whirs about
an opening or draws a baggy fleshsack close
and that in fact it meant

the world cannot I think be overstressed.

Sequel

The universe's ignorance of me is privacy.
I know the endangered meadow in a way
it will never know itself.

Must be the cosmos wanted something
to hear the splendornote
and find the fossil data,

to take an interest
in extinction events and ask
what pulsation is this

exserted from, what What.
I don't know about purpose,
the why of why

we're here, but we seem to witness
with a difference.
To think is to exercise

godheat. Haven't I been given
everything, my life?
I might as well revise

the opening to read
the universe adores me.
It leans. It likes. It feels

no one could fail in quite
the same way as I've.
It gives burnish

when what is worthy of it.
The cosmos must have wanted something
to provide ovation

and disdain and inquire
under whose auspices
comes applause and hiss

and ask whose modulations unscroll
in flowers so immoderate that many
fewer would be none the less

a form of excess.

Split The Lark

== Taste another snowflake, always flavored
with symmetry and quick. Taste it just by breathing.
Try the true north that is nothing
if not meat divine. He said

he'd seen a space shaped like a bowl
in the delicious snow, with brushmarks around it
as if someone had been sweeping
with a cypress limb. Some Mrs. Muskrat
from a golden book of storyland
where forest folk wear clothes.
Though these incisions were the work of wings.
And nearby, piled neatly on the crust, a lavish
moistly saturated maroon, were the intestines.
I guess it made him grasp enfleshment better,
the way flying glosses gravity
more vividly than lying down. It was something
about contrast, exotica, that livid turban on the snow.
"I want to kiss you but I feel nauseous,"

the poet gushed into the open mike,
and I quoted it later, amused and cruel.
I made it worse. Well, look
who's spilling now. At first he spared me
his discovery but I'm the kind who'd rather know.
It runs in the family. At least I've stopped thinking
knowledge is power and realized knowledge
is knowledge and power is
another thing entirely. Am I going to die?
my cousin asked her primary care physician.
It runs in the family. When Europeans visit
Michigan they sometimes ask

to feast on bear or moose. And there was that American
who went to France to eat a songbird, an ortolan,
which stands, they say, for the French soul.
The chef called them canaries, though ortolans
are buntings, a kind of bobolink, members
of the finch family, the size of
penises with gray-green heads. No two alike,
the snowflake platitude. The clouds' opacities
and glassy fields are textured as never
before, though on the whole, the winter
sky looks like the wrong side of a painting.
If I could only flip it, use my head or back to
lift it, if I had the eyes to
sift it, a proximate chromatic paradise
might come to light. The ortolans are caged in the dark

for weeks. Well, once upon a time
they were blinded with knives.
They feed constantly when deprived of day, you see.
After fattening, they're drowned
in cognac, plucked, fried, and presented
on their backs, swollen, shriveled delicacies
with wings folded and eyes bruised

open wide. *What's the Ugliest Part
of Your Body* as the old Mothers of Invention
tune asked. *Some say it's your nose—*
the celebrants drape large white cloths
over their heads for privacy and to enhance
the aroma of the liver and kidneys,
anus and brain becoming paste or pomade

      == When I opened the tiny bottle with my incisors
      the frangipani essence, bile
      yellow, spilled on my bitter orange skirt,

and what had been delectable
became a stink I couldn't stand or leave. Cruelty's

caused by ignorance, I used to think,
an unsolved riddle, like the one about the chicken
and the egg. Now I beg to differ. Now I think
you can prove the brutal
using split fields, fixed and moving
eyepieces, depth samples, horizon scans,
a wedge and a transparent plunger, you can shove
your fingers in the mess itself
and your mind will say but still and yet.
Will blend in white
until the visceral business turns pastel
then market it as peachy
patent leather edible bright wipes and send you

the nice invoice. Cruelty is convenient,
that's the thing. Ignorance is.
Bliss. I mean, I also have suffered
the wonderful to die. "Make sure your own
oxygen mask is fastened
before assisting others." In Beijing,
we interviewed the old men who walk
their birds every morning, swinging the cages
to mimic the sensation of flight.
They held contests to decide whose thrush sang best.
When I asked how they got their pets to sing they said
"We beat them. With a little stick. And did the U.S. troops
in Vietnam eat babies? We've heard this

is what you did." The American
savored the last meadow gasp of pollen
in the ortolan's lungs, the grit of millet
in its bowels, its final swig of sun
before its tissues filled with night,

grinding small to smaller till his molars met
the resistant cartilage and sinew, when, well,
I want to kiss you but
I feel nauseous says it best. Split the Lark—

and you'll find the Music—Place the Crystal
Gizzard on my tongue. I'll melt
the gothic arches of the not-body,
dissolve its feather pixels. I'll clean its clock,
receive. Lettuce leaf grass ripe unripe tomato
orange chocolate
beetroot white and whiteman's face
are tones plotted on the tongue-shaped graph
in *Colour: Why the World Isn't Grey*. Though of course it is

sometimes. I said punch-biopsy me
till the juice runs down my leg,
and they cut a scrimption of flesh
like the hole in binder paper except
this hole had depth, it was a tiny well
with a wicked wine confetti at the bottom,
it had death, I said, it was unsettling
to see so far into myself, creepy, I said,
and the doctors tried to hide
their smiles. You are going to die. Keep it simple, stupid,
which abbreviates to KISS. Keep the blech and yum
and ick. *The Ugliest Part?*

Some say it's your toes, grippage,
the opposite of on the wing.
The sky's gray emphasized by contrast
the swelter on the crust and the quiet felt
compensatory, felt remembering of
the shriek followed by the lift
of the carnivorous thing, the digestion of
a heaven ruminant with all

it had absorbed. "All the colours
formed by mixing real lights lie inside
the area enclosed by the tongue . . ."

== When I got to the bottom of the dish,
I saw what I'd taken
for peppercorns was in fact
ground glass. Did you know

any pigment ground infinitely small
will look sky blue? And isn't it cool
all snowflakes taste alike. Always flavored,
with no fat corners, with six-daggered ellipse.
Storm callus, blizzard skin, you taste
like death wish. Like marvelous
cold thing. That God does not apologize
is God's one sin. Well, it takes one

to make one, he said. It takes one
rooster and a million hens
to produce these free-range eggs.
The male chicks are suffocated, crushed,
decapitated, or gassed. He said this
at breakfast, provoking a loud
calm. Does the face look different
eating an ortolan, I wonder?
As it does speaking French
compared to, say, Chinese? As snowflakes
get their shape from water's shape
and the pigments in bile create
the blue of some birds' eggs.

"As the area outside the tongue
represents imaginary stimuli
we need not consider it further."
As long as I got a toehold, as long as I got

a piece of you. *Part of Your Body?*
I think it's your mind: where the moist and the warm meet
the cold and the pure
snow forms. The spring catalogues are full of hollow

chocolate hens and foiled chicks. Full of panoramic sugar
eggs with windows in their shells that let you see
the smiling Easter beast inside. See this
Baccarat bunny dish?
The head and spine lift off. The cover.
Yes, I see. Glass tastes like spring
water rising from a bed of chalk, flinty,
without body or bouquet. The microstructure
resembles rusted chicken wire. Going smaller,
at the quantum level, it's all oscillating

      == clouds. And I touched my lips
      to the tumbler, tuning out its flavor
      to relish what it held. The crystal

rabbit looked empty yet reflective:
you could catch your face in it.
Light turns incarnational upon entering
the brain. I filled mine with sweets and party favors.

Failure

The kings are boring, forever
legislating where the sparkles
in their crowns will be. Regal is easy.
That's why I wear a sinking fragrance
and fall to pieces in plain sight.
I'll do no crying in the rain.
I'll be altruistic, let others relish the spectacle—

as one subject to seizures of perfection
and fragments of success,
who planned to be an all-girl god,
arrives at a flawed foundering,
deposed and covered with the dung
and starspit of what-is,
helpless, stupid, gauche, ouch—

I'll give up walking on water.
I'll make a splash.
Onlookers don't want miracles.
Failure is glamourous.
The crash course needs its crash.

The Permeable Past Tense Of Feel

Let the barbaric flowers live, I'm living.
I'm liking the meadow blobbed with bird's-foot trefoil,
with earth-gall and the creeping wheatgrass
anciently known as felt. I mean nonelites
that live in disturbed soils, nuisance shrubs
whose fragrance exceeds exaggeration. Isn't it green.

These days everyone wants
two acres gated with herbicide. Everyone wants
to eat high on the food chain while—

Contain yourself. We need less
impervious surface per person

beginning with the mind.
Oh, the blisters sustained
while blaming others. The indignation of!
Only the sky has a right to such
disdain. Isn't it blue, my companion
animal said. And doesn't the body extend

into other endowed stuff. Feeling things
with blue irises and pink or brown
fleshy hairless ears
enrobed in fat and skin
that chew and breathe and joy themselves
by twisting, aerodynamic, when they jump.
That have soulweight and intestines.
That like Mozart,
which is played to calm them since calm
things are easier to kill.

Felt comes from "beat" and from "near."
== As hooks pass through, the fibers entangle
till our presence is a double-dwelling ==

        Why must I say they are like
     us whenever I say let them live? Speak eco-speak
     like eat no flesh and save the watershed, like
        maybe the whole blue-green.

How have I inconvenienced myself
in service to this feeling?
Felt is ideal for padding and sealing.
How have I left the earth
uncluttered with more me?

The inhabitant cleans and wipes,
eats and spasms. Cruelty exasperates
reason. At the top of its range,
ah is the only sound
the human voice can make. So felt
takes on the shape of flesh

        beyond resemblance
    into same, a thou-art-that that oscillates
   through pollen-throwing and clasping devices,
     ovaries and arms. So lid and lash
   close over iris and pupil, dissecting tables drain
       into our sweet spot.

The century heaves. Nowever. Who has time?
With primates to raise, important hearts
to hold down.

== When the box is full, hammers beat the felt,
which turns to present a new surface
before it's struck again ==

Lovers, givers, what minds have we made
that make us hate
a slaughterhouse for torturing a river?

As the prescribed burn begins, I see the warmth
sculpture rise higher, twisting from the base.
And though the world consists of everything

that is the case, I know
there must be ways to concentrate
the meanings of felt in one

just place. Just as this flame
assumes the shape of the flesh it covers.
I like to prepare the heart
by stuffing it with the brain.

Warmth Sculpture

Strange fits of passion! The author's hyperventilating
defense of geraniums in *First World Flowers*,
his overmodulation over "the dark period"
of tea rose breeding: what gets to others
sometimes leaves me numb. The blush and bliss of
sappy violins. The intensity of
sun on the stereo this morning
in concert with the strings—

If there were none attached, how unencumbered.
How trance in progress, everlastingness.
Since no one instant is
inherently different from another,
time has invariance. No strings.
Just the fluid ongoing
        no stain == tape == restraints
equal to the moment bleeding through.

        Hi Ma. I'm working on my book.
        Well, when this one's finished,
        don't do it again.
        My air conditioner quit, she says.

    Surfaces in contact
    do not touch everywhere.
    Just so == Just there.

When I survey the brightest reaches
in whatever direction I look it looks
the same. Only the silo distinguishes
our local sample from the remote.
Wrens live in the bullet holes.
How can I leave this to the unlove

of someone else? Unless I become
the opposite of connoisseur,
an immersant, reveler, welcomer
          of everything that is == that is

whale fossils with feet, the benefits of
making robots look less like people,
worm's brains, many body
problems, vinyl, chitin, nonelite greens,
unless I understand the secondary spongiosa
as a vaulted structure.
Books have been written!

Most people want blurbish blobs of praise.
Can I see each as a good thing of its kind
and love not only the stand-up sisters,
but the Group for the Suppression of Fushia?

At Kmart, a strange woman about 65
asked my mother for a ride. I said yes,
she says. Don't do it again! I interject.
I took her to her door and she tried to
give me a dollar as she got out.
Don't do it. Of course, I wouldn't
take it. Don't. I thought
you'd say gee, Ma, you're a good soul.

She greets those who are troubled and filled with lament.
May some find herein physically relevant
charms against extinction: don't

sit down in your new white linen suit,
use so many dictionary words,
shovel your own path or go on vacation
with you know who, drink only
grapefruit juice, check in without baggage

demanding a high floor, get to Mass too late
to get a vigil light or become a flash
in the pan—

Like you I long for fairness, some justice
that would let us live
in affirmation of eternity.
But what mind, what treetop research,
can rise high enough
for canopy studies of
the complete?

Recently I noticed the tiny small black blossoms
in the middle of the Queen Anne's lace.
I knew the red speck in the center,
but I didn't know of its unfolding.
It must be a bud that gives way to such
eldritch petals, really tiny violets.

Examine them today, not tomorrow.
Notice too the understory of rungs, the way
the flower hinges on green stays
as the century closes
and language strings consciousness to difference:

    a stain == tape == restraint ==

equal to the moment bleeding through
the unknown on both sides of the non-
linear equation. Strings squash abundance
which, face it, there's too much of.
They crunch invariance to flair
and highlight: the bundle, what was it,
my aunt brought each Monday,
white paper, bound with twine . . .

Hi Ma. I'm working on my book.
Do you have to do that?
Let this be the last. My fan
is on the blink, she adds.

When every moment's full of severance
what is left but to revel
in the delible
unlingering, precisely this
        goldening == dawn == silo == bird
singing contrapuntal above
the edgeless mono calm of
appliances, this century's ambient sound.

It isn't simplicity that epiphanizes me, it's
saturation, the maximal, interwoven
thrombosis and richness of
contributors to each morsel of
what-is: this density
in which all entities
exist. It works. It wilds ==

        The unknown on both sides of the *don't*:

forget to use your noodle, get knocked for a loop,
miss that show about the guy who gets
the paper the day before
and prevents a lot of accidents,
buy a lamp without a shade,
encourage intercourse with spirits,
go ashcan over tomato can,
have bouts, or fail
to give everyone my best red garters.

I give my best regards to those
who are cast down and beclouded,

those who pursue the miraculous
as a gesture of defiance,
heretics who worship in the chapel perilous,
those who live in the proactive *is*
to whom each moment is spacious
and those who gnash and weep alone.
May they find herein some charms
against excruciation and speak them
gently, disencumbered.

     When I survey the lightest reach of thee—

the intensity of string coloration in concert
with the sun's expansions on the silo's curve,
the unknown on both sides of the non-
linear brightness, the reciprocity swerving
everywhere exceeds my radiance threshold and life

forgive me! I have to close my eyes.

               Hi Ma. I finished my book.
               It cooled off nice.
               Thanks. I'm glad you like it.

Close

Books fight century fatigue. What a fast read
            she goes == he goes
            it felt like slow to me.
I was learning about volumes

solidified with resin and painted shut
with Brilliant White, a shade that happens
when titanium sharply creases light.
Maybe it should be called Somnia
or Snowblind. Maybe Migraine White.
As you'd guess, this library was some designer's
bright idea of how to hide
the pipes and vents. The book that said this said
they have authentic spines and bindings.
They can be moved or stacked.
They are real books in every respect
except that they are deeply closed
books. These are books slammed shut
on every mind they've known. To my mind,

this excess has been committed
to their detriment. That is, even a book
shoved under a wobbly table retains
its book-nature. A bibliophile like you
could replace it with your foot
and gobble down the book.
But the volumes I'm describing
require major disemboweling.
They'd have to be steamed open
like those mummy cases of papyri
that might prove to be more Sappho.
The linguistic blizzard beating still
inside them is none

of our business, their fictions
changed to valediction == the less said.
Their pages subsumed by white vises
like lilies overgrown by vases. Either marble
or the gilded monuments.
Forget ecstasy displays. Marble happens.
Given enough heat and pressure, rocks change
their textures and voila ==

marble. Is this too hard?
Maybe the contents are like rubies
stitched in flesh to keep the inside
of a warrior charged. And keep it fresh.
The wall behind the petrified library
became a relief of book edges, the part
with opening potential, done in
plaster, pressing back. Ghost books
the designer quips. Well books
are called all kinds of things. Light reading
                    she goes == he goes
                    what leaden prose.
Front matter, bastard title, perfect bound
or sewn. What use is it
to close it when it's in me, on parole.

Notes to *Sensual Math*

"Supernal": Page 142, the quote beginning " . . . I am not like /
them, indefatigable . . ." is excerpted from "Feed Me, Also, River
God" by Marianne Moore, published in *The Egoist*, III, August
1916. I'm grateful to Cristanne Miller for bringing this poem to
my attention.

"Turn: A Version": Pages 145–46, the dialogue quoted in the stan-
za beginning "said the River God, her father" is excerpted from *The
Sound of Wings: The Life of Amelia Earhart*, by Mary S. Lovell.
Page 149, the quote is from "Feed Me, Also, River God," by
Marianne Moore.